The House on the Hill
Ian Paul Lomax – The Early Years
ISBN: 978-0-9955729-3-5

Published by

i2i Publishing. Manchester.
www.i2ipublishing.co.uk

Dedication

I would like to dedicate this book, *The House on the Hill*, to my mother who brought me into this world. She was always there for me through difficult times and an ever-present shoulder to cry on. I will always truly miss her, until my last dying day and will love her always from the bottom off my heart. (R.I.P. Mum)

I must also mention in this dedication:

My sister Diane who was always there for me and was like another mother to me. (love you lots.)
My sister Pat who sorted out all the funeral arrangements for my mother and her fiancé Stuart who was a godsend for looking after the family.
My sister Denise.
My younger brother Stephen, who was always at the end of the phone when I needed him.
My brothers Mark and Derek.
Adrian and his wife Susan who helped me through these difficult times, (love you both lots.)
And finally, my friends Mark Slater, Fat Frank, Joe Cooke, Sheffield Paddy, Pete Stott, Andy Hart and Debra, Andrew Leigh (Pud) a true Bolton legend. Not forgetting all my friends from Chesterfield for accepting me as one of their own. There are too many to mention. Thank you all for being my friends.
And last but by no means least, Jack Walsh, my step-dad who meant more to me than my own father. Jack died in April 2013. (R.I.P.)
Ian Paul Lomax

Prologue

A bogeyman is usually an imaginary evil character but for me he was very real.

During my childhood, my mum would often say to me, "If you don't go to sleep, Ian, the bogeyman will come and get you."

My mum was right and the bogeyman was real, he was my father.

From the tender age of four, and probably earlier, I was beaten and dragged out of bed and slapped about the head and pushed under the water when I was having a bath. I lived in constant fear.

My mother was beaten all through her marriage to my father and I was constantly told by her to keep everything that happened in the family a secret, to protect the family name. Running away became the norm for me to get away from the constant beatings and the agony of watching my mother suffer. Christmas day was the only time I can remember my father being nice to the family and even having a laugh. Watching the clock, living in fear, listening to the door knock and frightened of what he would do was a constant nightmare. I constantly soiled and wet my bed and cried on my school desk and my education suffered because of the fear and the beatings.

As I grew up I became involved in gangs and football violence because I was rebellious and I thought violence was normal. having been brought up with it.

I finally turned the tables on my father and he was badly beaten for all the heartbreak and beatings my mother and I had endured.

When I was eighteen I left home. I couldn't bear to live in a house with so many bad memories. Everywhere I looked, I saw evidence of past violence; the blood stains on the wall, the hallway where my father tried to strangle my mother, the stairs where I was dragged down by my father, the bathroom where my dad used to put my head under the water and the bathroom mirror where my mum and I used to look at our bruised faces. This was where my mum used to put make-up on our faces to cover the marks so no one would know.

I finally left Derwent Road, the House on the Hill, for good.

Eventually, my mother too left my father and married a man called Jack Walsh. He sadly died of cancer in 2013.

My father died in March 1990 but before he died I finally made peace with him. At the funeral I stood next to his coffin and I cried. I asked him why he never said he loved me?

My mother died in hospital in July 2016, after a serious illness. Two weeks after her death I decided to write this book in her memory and to reach out to people who read this book who have suffered abuse, not to live in fear and run away and suffer like I did, but to go to the authorities and seek help.

Remember there is hope.

My final message goes to my mum. I will love you and cherish your memory always.

Your loving son *Ian xx*

Mercy

If you could look inside my life
And use my eyes
Would you pity me?
Could you see the desperate nights?
Hear my desperate cries
Locked away in a cage
And there's no way out
Begging for mercy
All I had was my mother's love and my father's betrayal
On my hands and knees
Begging for mercy
All I heard was my father's voice
All I received was his pity
Blood and tears and his anger
All I wanted was his love
I held out my arms in desperation
I cried out so loud
I wanted to be free from pain and sorrow
I wanted vengeance but it would cost me
The tables were finally turned
He paid for all the pain he gave me
I guess every story has a twist
I walked away, I guess mercy was the only way out.

Chapter One

My Mother - My Guardian Angel

My mother was born with the name of Irene Swales on the 15th February 1928. Her mother was called Minnie and her Father was called James (Jim to his friends.) She had a sister also called Minnie and four brothers called Harold, James, Alan and Alfred. She lived in Astley Bridge, Bolton in her early life on a street called Baxendale Street. She married her childhood sweetheart Sidney. (Sid to his friends) When she was 20 years old, in 1948, she gave birth to her first child, a girl called Denise. The same year, my mum followed Sid to the British Crown colony of Aden. Aden was located in the south of present-day Yemen. It was under British control from 1937 to 1963.

Aden consisted of an important port and its immediate surroundings covered an area of 192 square km (74 square miles).

Prior to 1937, Aden had been governed as part of British India (originally as the Aden Settlement subordinate to the Bombay Presidency, and then as a Chief Commissioner's Province). Under the Government of India Act 1935 the territory was detached from British India and was established as a separate colony of the United Kingdom; this separation took effect on 1 April 1937.

On 18 January 1963, the colony was reconstituted as the State of Aden within the new Federation of South Arabia. The federation in turn became the People's Republic of South Yemen on 30 November 1967, marking the end of British rule.

Sid was in the Royal Airforce and he had been posted there for two years. They both lived on the Airforce camp. My mum later had two other children, Diane and Derek.

Later, Sid was tragically killed in a roofing accident on Rose Hill Garage in Bolton in the mid-1950s.

My mum met my father in 1957 and moved to Didsbury in Manchester where I was born. She later had three more children, Patricia, Mark and Stephen. My uncle Jim bought a terraced house for the family in Lee street in Farnworth. During that time between 1960 right up till 1966 my mother was viciously beaten by my father along with me and other family members. She tried to stand up to him on various occasions and was punished for doing so. She always had bruises on her face and body and seemed to have a permanent black eye, such were the constant beatings she received. I heard stories that my dad was stabbed in the head and had suffered a head wound which needed stitches having been attacked by another member of my family. I also heard that my dad attacked my mother when she was attending to my baby brother in the cot. He attacked her from behind because my baby brother was crying and my mother split his lip with her wedding ring when she tried to protect herself. The family lived in impoverished times and my mum always did her best to put food on the table. She always put her children first, even after a severe beating. She still cooked, cleaned, ironed and looked after us which was a huge testament to the woman I called my rock. She still showered us with love and affection even though she was suffering at the hands of my father. I remember many times my mum would hold me in her arms sobbing and covered in blood and bruises.

Whenever we had any visitors, my dad would hide upstairs in his bedroom, out of the way, like the coward he was. My mother would cover the bruises on her face with plenty of make-up. She would carry on chatting with her friends as though nothing had happened and would cry her eyes out when they had gone.

I had seen her sitting in the front room even though it was freezing cold, because we couldn't afford any coal or wood for the fire, crying her eyes out for hours on end. She still protected my father and lied to her friends and neighbours whenever they asked about the bruises on her face so that she wouldn't embarrass the family. The only time my mum was happy was when my dad was working away or in prison (as I found out later.) She was so happy always listening to opera on the radio like Pavarotti, her favourable singer. She had a spring in her step she used to take us for walks to Farnworth Park where we spent hours at a time having picnics and generally having fun.

My mum used to invite friends and family around for a chat and cup of tea; something she didn't do when my dad was around as she was frightened of the backlash from him.

In 1966 we moved to Derwent Road. I remember it well. My uncle Alan, my mum's younger brother moved us and it was the year England won the World Cup.

My mother's suffering would intensify with the beatings she would receive. They would be more brutal and her injuries would become more severe. My father fractured her jaw which needed operating on in hospital. She also suffered broken ribs which resulted in another visit to hospital. A day wouldn't pass by without some kind of injury or mark on her face. My mother confided all her problems to Father Melvin our local parish priest who befriended her and persuaded my mum to see her doctor. His name was Doctor Preston. He tried his best to persuade my mum to leave my dad and go to the police but she never listened and still stood by my dad for the sake of her children. The doctor put my mum on medication. He prescribed Valium tablets for her to help her keep calm and sleeping tablets to help her sleep. I often saw my mum slip one in my dad's drink to knock him out so that she could have a bit of peace in her life. She did finally build enough courage to leave my dad and it was our local priest Father Melvin who would run us to the coach station where the driver let us all on for free after mum sobbed to the driver about my father.

We stayed at my sister's house in Brixham which was a small fishing village in south Devon. We didn't stay long, just a few weeks in total as my dad came and begged for forgiveness. So, there we were, back in the house on the hill. My dad would take my mum out and buy her flowers and shower her with all kinds of gifts. But it didn't last long. The beatings would start up again and the black eyes would appear on a regular basis. On a few occasions, I would see my dad chasing my mum screaming up the street and drag her home. Then things would stop for a while as my dad did another stretch in prison.

Denise and Diane left the house and moved away and lived their separate lives.

After my dad came out of prison he was very lucky not ending up back in prison again, for a very long time. It was only my intervention that stopped the inevitable by getting the police who stopped my father strangling my mother in the hallway in the house. I will never forget my dad begging on his hands and knees to my mum asking forgiveness and to my horror she told the police she didn't want to press charges. The reason she told me was, if my dad went to prison again she would lose the house and we would become homeless. She wanted to keep the family together.

Of course, the beatings would carry on. On one occasion, I saw my dad throw my mum down the stairs which resulted in her breaking her arm. The nightmare would come to an end when I was sixteen years old. By then I had finally built up the courage to stand up to my father by giving him a serious good hiding. He never touched my mother again after that. He took his anger out on himself by drinking bottles of sherry which my mum used to find all over the house.

Eventually, my mum fell in love with one of my dad's friends whom my mum had confided in. She finally left my dad in 1982 and married Jack in 1984. They lived happily together until he sadly died in hospital, of cancer, in April 2013.

My mum carried on her life with great strength after her loss. She went on holidays with my sister Diane to Benidorm in Spain where she spent six months of the year with Jack.

It all came to end when my mum died in hospital on the 8th of July 2016 of Sepsis (blood poisoning) which was caused by a bed sore which was badly infected. On the 22nd of July, I finally said good bye to her at the funeral. I cried a thousand tears; she was my rock, a shoulder to cry on. She was always my guardian angel who had always protected me against my father even though she often suffered the consequences.

She always tried her best to keep me on the straight and narrow and fought my corner in the courts for my rebellious ways. Many times, I would see her crying, not just because of my father, but because of me and the troubles I used to get into. That is something I will always regret. Throughout my life, she had always been there for me; always fed me and clothed me when I had been short of money. I will truly love her forever for always being there for me.

She was a mum in million, loved and cared by all. I thank her for giving me life and protecting me and standing my corner. She was the bravest of the brave. I will always love her till my dying day and cherish the memories we shared

Chapter Two

My father

My grandad and my grandma (little nanny).
The girl on the left is my auntie Ann, the baby is my dad and the girl at the front is my auntie Margaret

My father was born on the 23 February 1923. His name was John Minihane and he was known as Jack to many of his friends. He had two sisters, Margaret and Anne. His father was called John. He was Irish and was born in County Cork in southern Ireland. His mother was called Ann and was known as Little Nanny as she was so small.

I know very little about his past but what I do know about him is that he fought in the Second World War in the Royal Navy and in 1939 on the HMS Renown as a radio operator.

After the war, he worked at William Walkers in Bolton for several years. It was there that he had a major accident where he nearly lost his arm which was dragged through a cutting machine. This resulted in six months of skin graft treatment.

He was originally married to a lady called Connie and they had a son called Peter. She would eventually divorce him for cruelty after several years. They remarried in 1988.

He met my mother in 1957 and they both moved to Didsbury where I was born.

They would eventually have four children, Mark, Pat, Stephen and me.

My Uncle Jim bought a terraced house in Lee Street in Farnworth in 1960. It was a typical small terraced house built in the 1920s and was sparsely furnished. It was quite a small house for a family of seven to live in and with little money coming in we lived through very impoverished times.

My father was a jackal and a drunk. He was also a 'ladies-man' who would cheat on my mother on a regular basis over the years. My mother knew all this as she was told many times by her close friends. He was also a heavy gambler and wouldn't think twice of stealing my mum's purse or selling household items for his cravings. He was also very brutal and a bully and I nicknamed him the bogie man. He thought nothing of beating my mother and me and other members of my family and he did so on a regular basis, whenever it suited him. The only time we felt safe from harm was during the times he worked away (or so I thought until I later found out he did a stretch in prison for a stabbing incident in Farnworth.)

The house was sold in 1966 and we moved to Derwent Road in Highfield which was an estate in Farnworth. I called it the *House on the Hill*, not for the obvious reason of its location. I named it after a horror movie I watched on TV because of all the violence and fear in the family home.

My family lived in constant fear of my father and his continuous use of violence. He carried on with his brutality with a vengeance against me and my mother and my two older sisters who after a few years living there left and went their own ways.

My father did another stretch in prison between 1967 to 1968 for fraud and was very lucky not to do another one after trying to strangle my Mother in a doorway. It was only my intervention, ringing the police that stopped the inevitable. I remember seeing my dad on his hands and knees begging my mother to forgive him and to stop the police from locking him up. I knew this was the only way to stop the abuse. To my astonishment my mum dropped the charges and the police weren't too happy that she did so as they really wanted my dad locked up. She explained that it was because we would have lost the house and we could have ended up homeless and she wanted to keep the family together.

Because of her sacrifice, the beatings would carry on and resulted in my mother spending time in hospital on two occasions with a fractured jaw and cracked ribs, because of his brutality.

As for me, the abuse would carry on until I was 16 years old when the tables would be finally turned and I found the courage to stand up to him. He then received a bad beating which he truly deserved. It would be the last time he would ever touch me or my mother or any other family member again.

My mother would finally leave him in 1982 when she fell in love with Jack who she would marry in 1984. The marriage lasted until 2013, when he died of cancer.

My father would leave Derwent Road for the very last time in 1988 when he remarried Connie his first wife. They both lived in a small flat in Bolton. He carried on his drinking as he had a soft spot for sherry and as far as I know he carried on with his brutality to Connie until she died in 1990.

My dad died in hospital few months later but before he died he asked me for forgiveness and I accepted.

All the time I knew my father I only knew his bad side. I can never remember him saying to me that he ever loved me, not even once. I will never know the real reason why he beat me the way he did. All I ever wanted was for him to love me and be a father to me. I cannot remember my father ever holding me in his arms or showing me any kind of affection.

Christmas Day would be different, that was the only time I can remember when my dad showed any kind of love and affection.

These are the only memories I have with the father I called the bogie man.

Chapter Three

Brotherly & Sisterly Love

My brother Mark, on the left, with me

Even though I came from an impoverished background and times were tough (not just because of the abuse from my father) but because of the financial implications of my father being in and out of prison. This made money very tight. It was a time when my family all stuck together.

My brothers and sisters were an integral part of my growing up in the early days. I had three sisters and three brothers. Denise, Diane and Derek were my half-siblings from my mum's earlier marriage to Sid. Patricia, Mark and Stephen were my natural brothers and sisters.

Denise was born in 1948 and was the eldest in the family. She lived in Aden which is now called South Yemen for two years, with her parents. She was very attractive with shoulder length hair and very slim. She did her part in Lee street in Farnworth by working long hours in a factory which helped to put food on the table to feed all the family. She was a tough cookie and was another family member who faced my dad's wrath but apparently turned the tables on him by splitting his head open. She was the main one who stood up to my father on many occasions protecting the family. She loved Bolton Wanderers and followed them home and away and once courted the famous Roy Greaves who played for Bolton wanderers in the 1960s. She often quarrelled and had the odd sparring match with my sister Diane. I often took her side. She did move to Derwent Road for a while but moved away in 1969 to a place called Brixham in south Devon where she settled down and had four children. She still lives there to this present day.

Diane was born in 1950. She was quite pretty with long red hair and very petite. She often fought with Denise but, to be honest, always came out second best. They always argued over the simple things like washing the pots and who was drying them. It didn't take much of a spark to set them both off. She was generally very quiet and easy going but she could fight her corner. She was very caring and very protective of me, like another mother.

We used to go everywhere together when I was a young boy in Lee Street, always there when I needed her the most. She was an absolute treasure and I loved her to bits. She also suffered at the hands of my father but she often stood up to him especially when my dad picked on me and she often suffered the consequences. She moved to Derwent Road for a while but moved on to pastures new to a place called Loughborough in Leicester where she married and had two children and still lives there to this present day.

Derek was a sweet boy. When he was a young boy he suffered with meningitis which affected his brain and caused him to have epileptic fits. He was quite tall with short black hair and was as strong as an ox which I found out on a couple occasions when he chased me up the stairs and put his fist through the toilet door, after I had wound him up. He was a sweet and caring child and was always around his mother, helping her out, cleaning around the house. He always bought her gifts and he always cuddled my mum all the time such were his caring ways. As he grew older it was more difficult for my mum to look after him. He was on special tablets for his epilepsy. Derek ended up in a special home with specialist nurses who knew how to look after him. He is still living there to this present day.

Patricia was a very pretty girl and was twelve months younger than me. She was very slim with long blonde hair and was always being chased after by the local boys because of her good looks. She was very quiet and caring and always helped about the house. I got on very well with Pat and I can't ever remember saying a bad word against her although she did accuse me once of nicking her jeans from the line; something I always deny to this very day. My dad adored her and she was his favourite and as far as I know he never laid a hand on her. She stayed in Derwent until she was married and had three children and is currently living in Westhoughton in Bolton.

Mark was born in 1962 He was much smaller than me with long blonde shoulder length hair. We used to fight like cat and dogs as he used to wind me up no end. He ripped my Bolton Wanderers posters off the wall then ran down stairs laughing, hiding behind my dad. I lost count of the number of black eyes he received from me because of the constant aggravation he used to cause me. I remember chasing him over a mile from the golf flicks to my house after he threw a golf club at me.

Talking about golf clubs, we both went to Moss Bank and had a game of mini-golf. I was enjoying it till he threw a tantrum because he had lost. He slapped me across the face. Unlucky for him, I caught him and I hit him with the golf club on his hand and broke a bone such was the venom of the swing. I regretted it afterwards but he ran straight to my dad. I suffered a good hiding for my actions. He used to be an altar boy at the Lady of Lourdes church. When he was at school he wanted to be a priest which made me chuckle, with all the bad language he used to use. I don't remember my dad laying a hand on him and they used to get on very well most of the time. He lived at Derwent to the very end, until my dad moved out. Mark then moved away to pastures new. He never had any children and is currently running a successful business in Dublin.

Stephen was born in 1964 he was tall and very skinny with red hair. He was a very good natured lad and I don't remember ever saying one bad word against him. I was very protective of him and would never let anybody touch him or say anything against him. Like me he would always be fighting and arguing with Mark who would carry on with his trade mark and constantly wind Stephen up. Sadly, our Mark would always come off the worst. Stephen was another part of the family who my dad, as far as I know, never laid a finger on and he got on very well with him. Stephen was the last one to leave Derwent Road and he would finally marry and have three children.

Chapter Four

A place called Farnworth

The name Farnworth means 'the enclosure among the ferns' and according to a source dated 1787, the area was overrun with ferns. The earliest recorded name is Ffornword (from a land survey in 1282), becoming Ferneworth before it's modern name. In the 13th Century, the area was jointly owned by two landlords of Manchester and Barton, but this passed to several families, notably the Levers.

The industrial history starts in 1611 when George Hulton dug the first coal pits. By 1848 there were 20 pits in the area. There is a series of underground canals beneath Farnworth, dug in the early 1800's, which were used to transport coal to Worsley.

One of the earliest paper mills in Lancashire was built by the Crompton family in Farnworth. The first steam weaving mill was opened in 1828 by James Rothwell Barnes, later becoming a spinning mill, and the first iron foundry was opened in 1838. Central Park was opened on October 12th 1864.

Farnworth Streets started to be lit by gas from September 6th 1860. Thomas Brown from Kearsley, was the first lamplighter.

The first post office in Farnworth opened in 1836. Prior to that post was collected from Bolton. St John's, Farnworth's parish church, was consecrated in September 1826 by the Bishop of Chester.

From 1827, Farnworth Wakes started in September, an annual holiday period when a fair visits the town.

The River Irwell and the River Croal flow though Farnworth, and Crompton Lodges, which is reclaimed land from former mine workings, is a popular walking and picnicking spot.

Farnworth had a few famous people who were well known. Hilda Baker was one. For her part in the comedy serious 'Nearest and Dearest,' she co-starred with Jimmy Jewel.

Frank Finley was one of Britain's most distinguished theatre actors, though he became a household name through his starring roles in the 1970s hit television series Casanova (1971) and A Bouquet of Barbed Wire (1976). I used to see him around my home in Highfield and actually obtained his autograph a few times.

Alan Ball was another one I used to see knocking about Farnworth. He was a top footballer who played for Everton and Arsenal and England. He played in the 1966 World Cup final, when England won. The saddest part was that Bolton Wanderers turned him down for being too small.

Market Street will be remembered as the 'Monkey Run'. Loads of marriages (and mistakes) were made on it — it was where the lads met the girls. What they used to do was parade up and down between the Black Horse and Farnworth Park. There was even a 'posh side', the Black Horse side, and a 'rough side', which was (of course) the side where this story started. Either way, the intention was the same. Everyone had a good laugh, with the lads and girls eyeing each other up, cracking the odd joke and eventually, pairing off together.

People might think there are enough pubs now, but there used to be even more. There was the Bird i'th Hand, at the Black Horse end of town, the Bowling Green, next door to Woolworth's - this had an imposing entrance of two big pillars outside the door, just like those that Sampson, in the Bible, pushed down. At the end of King Street was the

Horseshoe Hotel. This was classed as a 'posh pub' and was knocked down in the late 1960s. The land where it stood is still derelict now after all these years. Another one was the Travellers Rest opposite the Horsham, which later became Edwin P Lees.

While on Brackley Street, there was a pub called the 'Rozerr Mop' by the locals. Asda and its car park swallowed this up.

People may be able to remember more. Smokies, Queens, Rose and Crown were the pubs I mainly went in. You were always guaranteed a fight in any of those pubs on a Friday or Saturday night and if you weren't from Farnworth you had to keep your mouth shut or you would end up tasting hospital food. And who could forget Blighty's a night club on Church Street facing the old police station. This featured some top line acts like Shawwaddy, Slade, and Tommy Cooper who was well known for being drunk on stage. Jerry Lee Lewis and Alvin Stardust to name but a few who attracted people from all over the northwest including our friends from Liverpool with their funny accents and haircuts. They didn't get on to well with the locals. Farnworth was always a close-knit community and was well known for being clannish with outsiders and it also had its fair share of nutters and characters which I found out to my cost on the odd occasion.

Farnworth was a rough place to live and you had to learn to handle yourself from a very young age. There were different gangs from various estates like the Highfield Boot Boys where I was a proud member, the Newbury Cave Men who used to tag along and then you had the Arcaders and the Green Laners. We used to all join together and fight against our arch enemies the Spillimies (Little Hultoners) and Boothstown who tried their luck once but got chased out of Farnworth and never came back again.

Farnworth was like the Wild West most weekends in the 1970s and was very lively. The police cells were always full which I sampled on the odd drunken Friday and Saturday night out. Every September there was the 'Wakes', or Fair, which came to Brackley Street. It was in two parts. The one for the adults was on some spare ground at the Albert Road end of Market Street. While a smaller one for the youngsters was behind the old King Street Baths.

So, there was plenty of fun for everyone. I certainly had mine. If I was not fighting with the 'Fair' lads, I was chatting up the local girls near the Walzer and having the odd cuddle on the big wheel. And yes, I did sample the odd knee trembler on my way back from the night out; well who didn't? We all used to be young once.

Farnworth is where I was brought up and went to school. I was proud of my identity I had magical times and I will always cherish the memories of a place I always called my home.

Chapter Five

Lee Street

My auntie Brenda on the left with my mum and my little brother Stephen

I came in to this world in Withington Hospital which was in Didsbury in Manchester in the year 1958. Didsbury is a suburban area of Manchester. It lies on the north bank of the river Mersey which is historically part of Lancashire. There are records that it existed as a small hamlet as early as the

13th century. Its early history was dominated by being part of the manor of Withington, a federal estate that covered a large part of what is now the south of Manchester.

Didsbury was described during the 18th century as a township separate from outside influence. In 1745 Charles Edward Stuart crossed the Mersey at Didsbury in the Jacobite march south from Manchester to Derby and again in the subsequent retreat.

Didsbury was largely rural until the 19th century when it underwent development and urbanisation during the industrial Revolution. It became part of Manchester in 1904.

Anyway, back to my story. I lived in Didsbury till I was two years old and my mum told me we lived in a two-bedroom rented flat and my Mum and Dad both worked in a pub to make ends meet. My dad worked as a cellar man and my Mum worked behind the bar until she fell pregnant with me.

Then we all moved to Lee Street, an old cobbled street in an old mill town called Farnworth, part of the borough of Bolton. Lee Street was your typical cobbled street with pre-war houses with outside toilets in the backyards. I very rarely visited the toilet after 6 o'clock. There was no lighting and I was too scared to go out in the dark. The outside toilet was in a brick shed; it was dark and cold, so my younger brother's red potty came in handy at the time.

The house we lived in was a three up and two down and was built in the early 1920s, it was a typical house of the era. My bedroom was quite large but very cold in winter; if I remember, in fact, the whole house was cold. There was no central heating at that time; we had a coal fire but we couldn't afford any coal so we had to suffer the results. We did gets bits of wood from the factory behind our house in the back street. Derek and I used to break up pieces of timber and my mum used to split it up with a hammer for the fire. Other than that, we used to sit with our coats on, it was so cold.

In my bedroom, there were three beds one each for me and my two brothers. They were Derek and Mark my younger brother. The wallpaper was quite plain with a flowered pattern and we had cream curtains. The floor covering was just a plain cheap brown carpet. It was so thin you could feel the floorboards when you walked in your bare feet. The boards used to creak at night-time and along with the wind it just sounded like a haunted house.

There wasn't much of a view out of the bedroom window as there was a large factory building in the back street. I and my brothers used to play there most days.

My sisters' bedroom was a bit smaller; there were just two beds where my sisters Diane, Denise and Pat slept. Pat slept with Diane. It was sparsely furnished with a large old fashioned brown wardrobe and two small bedside cabinets. The girls room was better decorated then ours. It had pink wall paper with cream flowers and nice cream carpet with pink curtains hanging on the window. My mum and dad's bedroom was quite pleasant. She had cream patterned flowered wallpaper with cream hanging curtains. There were a few pictures on the walls and a nice beige carpet.

The kitchen was very small with just enough room for a table and four chairs. The sink was old fashioned; it had two large taps one for cold and one intended for hot water which we never had as we used the kettle for hot water.

When it came to bath time my mum used to top and tail us in the sink, as we had no bath. There was a small pantry where my mum used to store the food.

The front room had a small brown couch with two wooden chairs, a brown thin carpet with a small beige rug, a glass cabinet in the corner and a small brown coffee table with a small black and white television on it. I very rarely ventured into that room as it was too cold even in the summer months.

At that time, in the early sixties in Lee Street, you didn't see much crime so people did feel safe and left their front doors open. But I did once see two young lads sneak into Mrs Bullah's house. They snatched her purse and ran off with my brother Derek in hot pursuit. He never caught them of course as his running skills weren't the best which was probably a good thing for him, at that moment.

Most of the people in the street were elderly and were very friendly and everybody knew each other. Every day you saw elderly women polishing their front door steps and mopping the paving stones in front of their houses. They would shout to each other across the cobbled street asking if their neighbours would like a cup of tea and a biscuit and a chat. It was the norm in those days; people were poor but they were a close-knit community.

Next door used to be a lady called Pat Greenalgh. She was a lovely woman in her 30s. I think she had a son called Alan who was the similar age to me and we used to play out together. He had a bit of a crush on my older sister Diane. Pat was always coming around for a chat which was good for my mum with all the troubles in her life. She was always knocking on our door for a couple of tea bags and a cup of sugar. I remember once Pat asked my mum if she would look after her brown Labrador as she couldn't afford to look after it. Knowing how caring my mum was she couldn't say no. I loved the dog and we called it Shandy. It was lovely dog, very friendly. It used to sleep on my bed most nights. Sadly, it got bad diarrhoea and died. I was heartbroken I really loved Shandy and that was the last time we ever had a dog.

In the street, I remember Mrs Bullah, an elderly lady who always gave me sweets if I went to the corner shop for her. Then there was a certain lady called fat Hilda. She must have been 25 stone. She couldn't walk far because she used to get out of breath. She was another one who used to knock on our door for any spare tea bags and a couple of spoons of sugar. It was around 1964 that we started to see more of my father again.

It was happier times for a while as he seemed to be a changed man. It was then that my younger brother Stephen was born. He was only small with red hair. He was very fragile and I was too scared to hold him but I loved him all the same.

I was very close to Diane she was seven years older than me. We used to go out and play together all the time. We used to go to what we called the chicken-hut. It was a big shed where the owners used to breed chickens but it was now left derelict. Diane and I made it a lot cleaner and patched it up as much as we could and we made it our little den. We always loved playing in it.

I remember a certain lad called Michael Haslam. He was a bit older then Diane but he wasn't quite right. He was always bullying me and he once tried to give Diane some sweets but they were tablets. Our Diane didn't fall for it and we both kept him at arms-length after this. We both had a good time playing in the run-down mill in the back street at the rear of our house, climbing the wooden rafters. We even made a swing tied to one of the roof rafters and we were always swinging on that until I fell off and broke my arm which put to end to our escapades in the old mill.

Diane and I still played out together and we used to venture further afield going for long walks and playing in the dell. It was just of Bradford Road. We used to collect bluebells, a flower which you saw only in spring. The dell was swathed with the colour blue on the grass banks and we used to spend all day collecting them and taking them home for my mum.

Not far from my house was a bowling green where we used to watch the elderly play bowls now and again. They would let us have a go. All that came to halt fairly quickly as I bowled one too fast and hit an elderly man on his ankles. He was hobbling about in pain. Diane and I did a quick escape and never went back there again.

Not far from our house there was a tyre fitting place. It was an old yard with large wagon tyres. We used to play in them for a while; it was all good fun.

I remember one time my brother Derek and I were playing in an old run-down derelict house on Campbell Street which was just off George Street; not far from our house. We made a small fire with some paper and some pieces of wood but unfortunately the fire got out of hand and we had to make a quick exit. We both ran up the back streets and we both stopped at the end of the street and to my astonishment the house was ablaze. It wasn't long before the fire brigade came and they soon had it under control. We both ran home and I remember my mum saying to me that I smelt of smoke. I just lied and told her I made a small fire in the dell to keep us warm and that was that.

I had good and bad memories of Lee Street; some I cherished and some I wanted to forget.

In 1966, the year England won the World Cup, it was time to move as the house was in poor condition and too unsafe to live in. We moved to 38 Derwent Road which I called the *House on the Hill.* A house that would become full of fear and violence just like a horror movie and would affect me for the rest of my life.

Chapter Six

The Rag and Bone Man

Older people will remember the rag and bone man with his horse and cart trundling down the cobbled streets shouting *Rag 'n Boannnnne,* and the children running out with bits of old clothing, for which they would be given a balloon, or if they were lucky a few pence. But what happened to this assortment of rags and why bone?

In later years, the term Rag and Bone man was given to anyone who plied the streets for recyclable items.

Bone was sold to a merchant who would crush it and turn it into 'Bone Meal' fertilizer or glue

Rags would be distressed and the resulting fibres made into a cloth which was made into cheap clothing. These were of very poor quality, but enabled the poor to buy clothes they would otherwise be unable to afford. The name of the cloth was 'Shoddy', a name which is now used as a term to mean 'of poor quality'. Every Wednesday night the rag and bone man used to come into the street where we lived. This was Lee Street which was part of an old cobbled estate. The cart he used was old and black and it was pulled by a large white shire horse. He would ring his bell and shout 'rag and bone' at the top of his voice. I got to know the rag and bone man very well. He was called Paddy for the obvious reason that he was Irish and he came from Dublin. He was very pleasant; a man in his early 40s, well he looked like that as he never told me his age. He was stocky and well-built with a poker face and long black hair. Now and again he would let me jump on his horse and cart and ring the bell as we went around the cobbled streets where I lived. I used to look forward to seeing him every week and every Saturday night.

He would also come around our street selling cockles and muscles which Paddy used to let me sample for free now and again. Anyway, back to the serious stuff. In the early 1960s people were very poor. They ate what they could afford or even sold household items to put food on the table. Brothers and sisters would sleep in the same bed and we were no different from the rest. These were hard times, so when paddy came down our cobbled street ringing his bell and shouting *'rag n boannnnne'* people would come out of their houses and try to sell their cast-offs for a few pence. It was a sight to see. All the old women wore their shawls and queued up at the side of the cart. My mum used to wait until they had all gone and root through the clothes so see if there was anything she liked. Paddy always let my mum have them cheap as she always made him a cup of tea. After all, we classed Paddy as a friend of the family. This used to be a regular thing every week with mum, she would always barter with Paddy for the clothes she wanted. She said that we were always smartly dressed. After all, we did live in impoverished times but it still made me chuckle. In those days, it was a close-knit community and if any of our neighbours' younger children grew out of their clothes, they were passed on for good use elsewhere. My mum was always going to jumble sales looking for clothes at bargain prices; it was just the way it was in those days as times were very hard.

Back to Paddy; we became good friends for a while until he found pastures new. There was a tale going around that his horse had died and that he went back to Dublin and lived the rest of his life as a drunken tramp. I will never know the real reason but he was a character was our Paddy.

Chapter Seven

Impoverished Times

On a Friday night, we had a special family treat. My mum used to send me to the local chippy with a big bowl for chips and scraps (fish pieces) and peas. I felt like Oliver Twist. *"Please sir can I have some more?"*

Times were hard in the early sixties. Money was very scarce. If your parents weren't working you depended on family relations or even your neighbours for hand-outs. My father was in and out of prison and if he did do any work, he gambled it or spent it in the nearest pub. Such was the bastard he was.

In our household, it was so cold we used to sit in chairs with our coats on, wrapped up in blankets or cuddled up to each other to keep warm in the winter time; praying to God for the summers to come early. The fireplace was as bare as our kitchen pantry. I don't remember ever seeing the coal man coming to our house at any time. Having a bag of coal was like winning the lottery today. Diane and I used to bring timber out of the factory behind our house and my mum would break it up and make a fire. The whole street had the same idea and they were like locusts. They stripped the factory timbers bare. Sometimes my mum put some of our old clothes on the fire to keep the fire going and the whole family had it in turns sitting around the fire for a warm. For breakfast, all the family used to sit around the table for our usual slice of toast and a cup of tea and if anybody was off colour and didn't feel well, it was all ways me who asked, "can I have it please?"

It was always my dad who got the first refusal and he always replied with the same answer, "Don't be bloody greedy lad," and he would eat it all himself.

Usually for dinners my mum would make us all sugar butties (sandwiches) which I detested but I ate them all the same as the hunger pains used to kick in. For our teas, it was usually potato hash with red cabbage and if we were lucky some of my mum's homemade currant cakes, which were delicious. Sometimes fat Hilda from the corner house used to bring us six eggs around to the house, as she had three chickens in her backyard and my mum made us all scrambled eggs on toast.

Now and again in Lee Street the neighbours, on a Saturday, used to set up tables in the street and everybody contributed bits of food and homemade lemonade and we used to have a party till late in the night. Mrs Bullah was my favourite; she made the best home-made lemonade I had ever tasted. She always made sure I had a bottle, bless her!

At the end of Lee Street there was a corner shop. It was mainly groceries and fruit and on the counter the owner always had a toffee jar for whenever my mum sent me to the shop for a tin of corned-beef for the potato hash. Jack, the shop keeper used to give me a couple of sweets for free and now and again if any of the apples or bananas were going off, Jack used to put them in a bag and give them to me. I used to skip home on the cobbled streets and give them to my mum to share out.

Bath times, what bath? My mum used to strip me down in the sink and pour warm water over me then wash me down with a flannel and the old green block of fairy soap which used to bring me out in a rash.

Clothing was always a problem for me. I was only small and skinny and finding the right size for me was a major problem (not in the clothes shops as I don't remember my mum ever entering one) but for the rag and bone man as I was very small for my age. The clothes I had to wear were always too big and some of the jumpers I used to wear used to keep my knee caps warm as they were always two sizes too big. The sleeves sometimes nearly touched the floor and my mum used to roll them and turn them up until you saw my hands. Many a time I used to wear my older sisters' knickers because I didn't have enough underwear and it was the same with the socks. Sometimes I wore different colour socks and my mum used to say to me that nobody could see them. "Ian your long pants will hide them."

All the neighbours in our street used to pass down all their children's clothes to one another and whenever we played out in the street you could hear the kids' remarks, "Ha Ha, they used to be mine, them!" And I remember one kid pointing at me and saying that he pooed in the pants which didn't go down too well with me.

Then I would run home sobbing and tell my mum but she would reply, "Don't be soft Ian they have been washed."

Whenever I got nits I used to dread it. I hated to think creepy crawlies were in my hair but it wasn't that that scared me to death the most it was my mum. She used to sit me down on a newspaper and comb through my hair and pull them all out and then put them on the newspaper. I wasn't just head-sore but I used to have to watch them crawl all over the newspapers till she finished checking my hair for the bloody nits. I used to have nightmares thinking about them. I used to scratch all night at just the thought of them.

Talking about newspapers, they used to come in handy. If we ever ran out of toilet-paper, we had to use the newspaper when we went for a shit. It always left the newspaper print all over my bare cheeks.

Times where difficult but we still had fun. Like my Grandad used to say in his broad Bolton accent, "Ee bah gum lad times, were bloody hard ".

Chapter Eight

Childhood Fun and Games

In the 1960s and 1970s children were expected to go outside and play. Such play often did not involve much in the way of props. The play relied on imagination and energy. Many a mother simply said, "You kids go outside and play," and the kids did.

One of the earliest games I played was hopscotch. I used to play with the kids in my street on the old cobbles in Lee Street. My mum bought us some chalk from the corner shop which was only cheap in those days. Starting on two feet, we'd have to hop on one foot for a couple of blocks, then get a 2-footed respite, then continue again to the 2-footed block on the other end. Developing both balance and rhythm were critical to success at hop scotching. Girls seemed especially good at it, and singing or chanting while doing so was not only accepted, but encouraged. The chalk did come in handy sometimes scribbling on walls on the house fronts as kids do. Writing your names and if you were lucky a girl's name.

I remember my fist kiss I was 4 years old. It was with a girl from my street. I think she was called Denise. It was probably my first crush. She was a year older than me. I scribbled our names all over the cobbled streets and on the odd occasion on Fat Hilda door which didn't go down well as she threatened to tell my mum and dad.

Another game was 'Kick the Can' and required only a used can Mum provided from the kitchen, often an empty soup can. The game was usually played in our street, and could involve any number of kids. It was soccer before any of us knew what soccer was.

RED ROVER was a group activity. You needed at least six kids to play it, and eight or ten worked even better. Each side lined up facing the other, clasping hands with their teammates. One team would send a runner at the other team. The runner would crash in between two of the other team's players, where their hands met. The runner tried to break the hands apart, while the defending team tried to stop the attack and catch the runner. If the runner broke through, they grabbed a player from the other team and took them back to join their team. If the runner didn't break through, such runner was captured by the team that stopped them.

'Mother, May I?' That game involved one person exercising mother's powers, while other kids asked permission to take steps toward the mother figure. It sounds kind of silly, and looking back, I suppose it was. "Mother, may I take a baby step?" The answer might be "yes, you may." "Mother, may I take a giant step?" The answer might be "no, you may not." It was a completely arbitrary game, but we played it anyway.

As you got older you got more adventurous and you took more risk. 'Jumping rope' could be either a single or group activity. If there were at least three kids and a rope, two could swing the rope around, and the other kid or kids could run into the swinging rope and jump. Singing an appropriate song was encouraged. If one was by himself or herself, a single jump rope would do. I remember swinging on a rope and the branch snapped in the dell. Luckily for me I fell into the stream but I ended up with a badly bruised bum for my troubles and I couldn't sit down for days.

'Knock a door run' was a game I loved playing but that ended abruptly after I was punished for waking somebody up who was working nights. I was pinned against the wall and smacked around the head a few times but I did get my revenge. When I brought some fireworks at my local shop, I fired a few rockets at his window and pushed some bangers through his letter box and they exploded with a loud bang.

'Truth or dare' was a game I played a lot with my friends, for a laugh. I remember one time I was playing with Frank and Mick and Leslie in Eskdale Grove near my house in Highfield. We asked each other in turn to tell the truth or dare. It was always a dare with us. I asked Mick to say the alphabet backwards as fast he could and I laughed my socks off as he struggled. Frank dared Leslie to take her top off which she did showing her ample breasts in a white bra. It was now my turn. Leslie laughed and said take all your clothes off and run up the street.

I was up for anything as Leslie found out in the months ahead. It was 6:30 in the evening and it was still pretty light. I casually took all my clothes off and ran up the street and when I returned to pick up my clothes, Leslie and Frank had run off with them up Derwent Road. I was naked and I had nowhere to hide. To my embarrassment, a neighbour saw me. It was Mrs Worthing, my mum's friend. She came out with a towel to cover my modesty up and told me to go home before I got into serious trouble. I ran like a bat out of hell, clutching my towel till I got to my house. I knocked on the side door and luckily for me my mum answered it. I told her what happened and she burst out laughing and told me to get some clothes on and she shouted to me as I was running up the stairs that I was lucky my dad was out otherwise my bottom would have suffered with his belt.

'Trick or treat.' I always looked forward to. Throughout Britain, Halloween had traditionally been celebrated by children's games such as bobbing for apples in containers full of water, telling ghost stories and the carving of faces into hollowed-out vegetables such as swedes and turnips.

These faces would usually be illuminated from within by a candle, the lanterns displayed on window sills to ward off any evil spirits. The current use of pumpkins is a relatively modern innovation imported from the United States, and we can also extend the same debt of gratitude to our friends in America for that quaint 'trick-or-treat' tradition! My family was quite poor but my mum did try her best. She dressed me up like a witch, put a bit of make-up on my face and she gave me a small bucket to put all the toffees in. Frank and I, really looked the part. He was dressed up like the devil. He had all the gear and his face was painted. We knocked on a few doors and as usual some couldn't be bothered to answer. We did get the odd cake and toffees. One particular door I knocked on, the light was on upstairs so I kept knocking. Next minute the top window opened and this bloke poured a bucket of water over me then shut the window laughing. I was soaked to the skin. Frank was laughing his socks off. I didn't find it amusing so I picked a rock out of his front garden and threw it through the man's window and we both did a runner laughing as we ran up Derwent Road. I was always up for a laugh and I did anything for a dare. I have the scars to prove it. I was mischievous but I just thought I was a loveable rogue. All these activities kept us healthy, developed our bodies, gave us rhythm, strength, and enhanced hand and eye coordination. Childhood obesity was rare in those days although we ate a lot of sugar and fat.

Kids playing outside and using little in the way of props was one of the things parents and kids of the 1960s and 1970s really got right.

Chapter Nine

Family Holiday

It wasn't all bad times. In the early 1960s a family holiday was a rarity as money was very tight. My dad wasn't around and I was told he was working away but it wasn't till I was older that I found out he was in prison.

My first trip to the seaside was with my older sister Denise and my younger brother Mark together with her friend Eileen and it was a trip to Southport. But Blackpool was my favourite destination. I remember one bank holiday morning my mum waking me up and saying, "get up Ian we are going to Blackpool for the day."

I thought she was joking but she kept saying with a big smile, "Get up, we have to catch a train soon."

I jumped out of my bed and I cuddled my mum and I said thank you. She rubbed my hair and said it was my treat. I was so excited I looked through my bedroom window and it was quite sunny.

My mum washed and dressed me. I remember I was wearing a blue shirt with blue shorts and a pair of brown sandals which I didn't know at the time belonged to my younger sister Pat. I was seven at the time and the year was 1965. We had our usual breakfast at the table. Jam on toast and porridge which I disliked. I always thought it was too thick and lumpy as there wasn't enough milk on it. I always struggled to swallow it.

Around the table were my sisters Diane and Denise who sat separately as they were all ways fighting with each other. Then there were my brothers Mark and Derek. Stephen, who was only two at the time was sitting in the pram. At the head of the table was my mum who was giving out her usual orders to eat up and don't waste anything as money was tight.

Denise and Diane helped my mum with the food and drinks for the picnic to take to Blackpool. We had chicken and chips which were already cooked, biscuits, fruit, homemade cakes which were always made with currants, jam sandwiches and sugar butties. And the usual flask of tea of course together with lemonade. Finally, there were our swimming costumes just in case it was warm enough to go paddling in the sea.

We were all dressed and ready. It was a real family day out. My sister Diane pushed Stephen in the pram; Denise, Pat, Mark, Derek and I, and of course, my mum.

We all walked from Lee Street to the train station in Bolton which was about 4 miles from our house so it took us just over an hour. It soon passed as we all had a laugh on the way down and watched my mum telling off my sister Diane and I for the usual falling out with each with other.

We arrived at the train station about 10.30 am and there were hundreds of people queuing up to buy tickets. I looked around and there were plenty of children with buckets and spades, parents with prams and the odd grandparent wagging their finger at some poor old child who looked frightened to death.

We finally got on the train with was packed to the rafters. I couldn't breath and my mum kept squeezing my hand and smiling at me to let me know she was there. There were plenty of children crying on the train. They were obviously scared as we were all squeezed together like sardines.

It was a long journey which took nearly two hours and it was a hot summer's day which didn't help matters.

We finally arrived at Blackpool I began to get very excited. It was my first trip there and I had heard so many stories about the beaches and the arcades and the donkey rides and of course the famous Blackpool tower from my school friends who had already visited the place. We walked out of the station and passed all the shops. I had never seen so many. We carried on walking and we headed for the promenade. Along the way, we passed hotels and bars. There were hundreds of people on either side of the road. In the background, I could see a large tower which seemed to be high in the sky. I pointed it out to my sister Diane and she said it was Blackpool Tower. We finally arrived at the beach. You couldn't see the sand as there were thousands of people sunbathing and children building sand castles with their bucket and spades. I could see the sea which was deep blue in colour and it seemed to stretch for miles.

We finally found a spot where we could all sit down. My mum pulled a blanket out and we all sat down on that. Out came the refreshments. I was thirsty and hungry by now. A jam buttie and lemonade went down well. Now and again you would see a seagull swoop down like a German dive bomber and try to get the food out of our hands. As usual Diane and Denise where arguing over something or nothing and it wouldn't take long before my mum started to wag her finger at them which was enough to stop them on the spot.

The rest of the day went off peacefully. We all larked about on the sand. I kicked over a few sand castles which didn't go down to well with some of the other kids' parents. Diane and Denise paid to go on a donkey ride which didn't turn out to their expectations. Diane's donkey wouldn't move no matter how she tried by kicking and shouting at it. It just stayed static in the sand. As for our Denise, her donkey ran off in to the sea and she fell off and got a good soaking which brought a roar of laughter from the people on the beach.

She wasn't the only one to get soaked I ran into the sea in my clothes. My mum wasn't amused. Later on, we all went into the arcades. They were packed to the rafters. I was amused at watching people putting money in the slot machines and now and again you would hear trickles of money coming out of the machines. I was fascinated. I wanted to have a go to try to win some money but I got the usual answer off my mum, "We don't have money to burn Ian." This was an old saying in Lancashire. We did all get a treat, however, an ice cream or a stick of rock.

We walked along the promenade from one end to the other and looked in the souvenir shops. We never bought anything; we just looked all the same. It's what we call window shopping today; you look but you don't buy. I wanted to go into the Blackpool Tower but because we had a big family we just couldn't afford it. We finished the day going to the amusement park where we had a couple of rides. Over all we all had a fantastic day out in Blackpool; a childhood memory which I always cherished.

Chapter Ten

The Bogie Man will get you

When I was little my mum used to talk about the Bogie man. She used to frighten me to death. She always said, if I didn't go to sleep he would come and get me.

I always thought of the Bogie man as some kind of demon that creeps about in the night.

Little did I know the nightmare would come true and it wouldn't be the Bogie man who would come to get me, it would be my father.

My father was only small and slim with short black hair. He was handsome but he had dark secrets. He loved his drink and gambled and he was always a bad loser and he used to take his losses out on me and my mother. I remember my father being in and out of my life when I was a young child. My mother used to tell me he was working away but it wasn't till I was older that I found out he was in and out of prison.

My nightmare began in 1962. I was just four years old and we lived in Lee Street Farnworth.

For whatever reason, I was very scared whenever my dad came near me. I used to shake with fear and for a good reason. Whenever he came home drunk, which was often, he used to scream at my mum to put his tea or supper on. This was when I saw him for what he really was a bully, demonic and a monster in my eyes. On one occasion, I couldn't sleep. I heard some shouting downstairs. It was about 12 pm. I sneaked downstairs and saw my dad arguing with my mum. He was very angry and was shouting out loud and I was very surprised that the rest of my family hadn't heard him. I watched in horror as he punched her in the face and grabbed her by the hair to drag her across the kitchen floor. I shouted at him to stop but he carried on kicking her around her body. My mum was screaming for him to stop. I just ran over to my dad and I kicked him in the leg. He turned around and punched me in the face knocking me on the floor. I was screaming and crying out in pain. My mother screamed at him to leave me alone. I just looked at him in pure terror and at that point my dad turned the kitchen table over and walked out of the kitchen and upstairs into his bedroom. My mum was covered in blood and so was I. She wiped us both clean then without a word she took me upstairs and put me back in my bed.

This wasn't the first experience of seeing my dad's anger and it wouldn't be the last. I didn't sleep much that night not because I was in pain but because of the fear of my dad coming in my room. Every time I heard a noise or the stairs creaked I hid under the bed clothes. I was petrified. It was the first time I wet the bed which I would carry on doing well through my early teens. My mum used to put terry nappies on me to stop me wetting the bed and soiling my pants.

The second time I saw my dad's anger was when I was sitting in the kitchen with my mum having a laugh. I heard the front door open and bang shut and my dad staggered into the kitchen. He was obviously drunk and his speech was slurred and it was only 2 o'clock in the afternoon. I remember I was sitting on the kitchen table playing with my mum. For no apparent reason my dad just came over, pushed my mother to one side and punched me hard on my nose. The force was so great that my head hit the back of the wall and blood was pouring out of my nose. I will never forget the look on my father's face, it was pure hatred. I remember crying furiously and my mother's look of fear which still haunts me to this day.

My mother and I weren't the only part of the family to suffer. I had seen my dad's anger at my sisters Diane and my older sister Denise on various occasions.

For a while the abuse seemed to stop and there was a bit of normality in the household. My dad wasn't around and I was told he was working away but I know now he was in prison for a while.

When my dad was back on the scene the abuse started again. He carried on knocking my mother around and bullying my sisters. Once my mum was on the top of the stairs and my dad threw her down stairs, he then turned his anger on me and punched me so hard in the stomach I yelped out in pain as I couldn't breathe. On another occasion, he threw his dinner at my mum's face and cut her eye open. My dad was now out of control the violence was getting worse and came to head when my dad was choking my mum. The screaming was so loud that Pat, our next-door neighbour, started banging on the door. It was then my dad stopped. I opened the door and Pat came in and shouted "what's going on?" My dad just walked out and it was then Pat held my mum in her arms and begged my mum to call the police but she just told Pat it would be ok.

I carried on wetting the bed at night and on some occasions, I would soil my pants it was obviously affecting me. I was starting to come out in nervous rashes but my mum never took me to the doctors in fear of my dad ever finding out. The violence was intense at times and relentless and there were no holds barred with him. He didn't care if it was a woman or a young child he hit. Such was the state of his mind!!! My mum seemed to have a permanent black eye as the violence continued. He was a monster and he was the Bogie man who was my nightmare in my dreams but it was all based on reality. The abuse carried on well into my late teens but one day the tables would be turned and the abuse would come to an end but for now the nightmare would continue.

Chapter Eleven

The House on the Hill

The year was 1966 and it was time to move on as the terrace house we lived in was becoming a little run down because of the cold and wet weather. The house was very damp which wasn't good for our health. The outside toilet was on the verge of collapse so it was unsafe to go in, especially at night time as there wasn't any lighting. I never ventured in there and my younger brother Stephen's potty came in very handy.

Pat, our next-door neighbour had already moved on to pastures new. Poor old Mrs Bullah had died, and so had a few of our neighbours as most were very elderly. We would never see Fat Hilda again after we moved and as far as I know she stayed till the very end until they knocked down all the terraced houses and built new houses on site.

I missed Lee Street and its old cobbled streets and Paddy the Rag and Bone man, the likes of him would never see again. The elderly women cleaning their front steps and the comraderie we all had in the street.

I didn't miss the dark and macabre nights with my father but Lee street had a big character and I did miss the old place.

I remember the day well when we moved. My uncle Alan, my mum's younger brother moved us in an old white pickup truck. It didn't take us long to load our personal items and furniture and move them to Derwent. Our house was quite sparsely furnished anyway. It only took only a few trips and would take twice as long to furnish the house and over twelve months to completely carpet it. The house was of new and recent construction. I remember my mum and I would walk up from Lee street a few times watching it being built.

The house had a large front garden and a small rear one at the back which was fenced off.

The kitchen was quite small with a few cupboards and a pantry which was quite cold. It was here she put all the fresh food and the milk. The back room wasn't very big really; it had a coal fire with a surround! We would take turns sitting on it so we could keep warm. We had a black and white telly with a metre on the back. It was what they called 'pay for view.' If we didn't have any coins to put in it that was that. We had to find other things to occupy ourselves. We had an old fashioned brown suite with two chairs. The curtains on the window were white with red flowers. Most of the other decor was cream. We had a small hallway from the kitchen to the front door.

The front room we called the lounge was where my dad was usually located. I very rarely frequented it, if my dad was in there. The decor was white walls with patterned flowers. Inside there was a green settee with one extra chair and a small coffee table, and a cream jar with some artificial red roses in. Also, there was the odd sprinkling of pictures on the wall.

Upstairs there were three rooms; a small box room where my two sister Diane and Denise slept. There wasn't enough room to swing a cat; just enough room for two small single beds. The curtains were pink to match the decor.

In my room, we had three small single beds for my two brothers Mark and Stephen and for me. The decor was pretty simple, just plain white walls with cream curtains. On my side of the wall I put up posters of my beloved team, Bolton wanderers and Mark put posters up of his favourite football team on his side of the wall. Mark was a staunch Everton fan to my dismay and this caused the odd fight now and again arguing about which team was the best. He was always a wind-up merchant and suffered the consequences for it throughout our childhood. The side street from my house was called Eskdale Road and across the road from where I lived were just fields at the time before they developed it.

At the top of Derwent road there were the police houses where the infamous Sergeant Swann lived with whom I would cross paths many times as you will soon find out later. We had a few shops on Highfield, the Cooperative, a chip shop, Flanagan paper shop, a fruit shop and a post office. There was a large pub called the Flying Shuttle. It would become one of the toughest pubs in Farnworth. It was here my dad and I would learn our fighting skills as trouble kicked off there almost every night. There were plenty of estates around where I lived and plenty of fields where, on the odd occasions, I would go camping or play football.

I would eventually call the house where I lived, *The House on the Hill*. This was after a horror movie I once watched. It was a house that was filled with pure evil and things that would creep in the night but it wasn't the bogey man, it was my father who haunted my House on the Hill.

Chapter Twelve

New Home, More Violence

I was settling down in my new house and I starting to get used to the surroundings nearby. I made a few friends like Frank, Mick and Liam. I was eight years old at the time. I was only allowed to play in the street at that age and I wasn't allowed to venture out far. I was always playing football on the grass verge or in the street. We used to use our jumpers or coats as goal posts. It was fun and for a while I had a smile on my face. The smiles would soon suddenly stop and the beatings and fear would return with a vengeance. My father would just start picking on me for little things, or even nothing. I did my best to avoid him, but if I couldn't, he would just start yelling at me.

I was set a rule that I only ever went into the kitchen for food, at certain times – and if I missed that slot, I went without – but I was too afraid to go downstairs in case he chased into the kitchen after me as he always did. Bawling at me, backing me into the corner until I was whimpering and crying, he would just laugh at me and walk away, satisfied by my distress.

Despite all of this, the hardest thing for me was seeing how he behaved towards my mum. He would shout at her about me and they would have huge arguments and I just couldn't handle it.

I was shut up in my room, hearing his aggression, fearing for my mum's safety, and it felt like it was all my fault. My name was brought into everything and he made sure I heard every word. I never liked to come home from school. I hated my dad. I was always having accidents in bed I couldn't stop wetting the bed and not surprising with all the abuse since I was little.

One night I had to go to the toilet. I accidentally soiled my bed and I was covered all over in it, the smell was horrendous. I put the light on as I was always scared of the dark and for obvious reasons when you had a father like mine. I was in the toilet when a heard the bedroom door opening. It was my father he came straight in and started to shout abuse at me, "calling me a dirty bastard." He knew I was scared and that I was crying. I was shaking. I was petrified. He grabbed my hair and pushed me to the floor and he kicked me and punched me repetitively. My mum saved the day and got in between us pulling him off but not before he punched her in the head and she banged her head against the wall such was the power of the punch. My dad just muttered something under his breath and walked out and went down stairs. I was crying my eyes out when I saw a trickle of blood at the side of her head. I picked a towel up and put it under the tap I then put it on the side of my mum's head to stop the bleeding. I felt the lump on the side of her head and it felt like the size of a walnut. My mum picked herself up and even though she was clearly suffering she undressed me and washed me down in the bath. She gave me a cuddle then put me into my bed then she got in beside me and she cuddled me all night. I felt safe when I was held in her arms. It wasn't too long before I fell asleep.

In the morning, I woke up and my mum wasn't there. I could hear voices downstairs. I hid on the top of the stairs. I could clearly hear my dad shouting at my mum. I was shaking with fear. I went to my sisters', Diane and Denise's room to try and wake them up as I was scared but they were fast asleep. I ran back into my own bedroom and hid in the bed under the blankets shaking with fear. I wet the bed once again as I was frightened and I was too scared to go to the toilet.

After a short while I got up and hid again on top of the stairs but it was very quiet. I sneaked down the stairs, step by step making sure I didn't make the stairs creek or make a noise. When I reached the bottom of the stairs I crept slowly into the kitchen. It was there that I saw my mum sobbing with her head in her hands. I looked in the front room and I couldn't see my dad. I peeked around the kitchen door and I couldn't see my dad in the back room. It was then I felt safe. I tapped my mum on her shoulder and she just lifted her head up and wiped her eyes. Then she looked at me and saw that my pyjamas were wet. She undressed me and took me upstairs and then stood me in the bath and washed me down without saying a single word. She was still crying and I felt so sorry for her, I loved her so much.

She tried her best to disguise her feelings but I always knew she was suffering and was so unhappy but she always carried on regardless. I just couldn't understand why my dad was so angry with us all the time and did what he did. At the beginning, I thought there was something wrong with me. It was only when I got a bit older that I realised he was just sadistic.

My dad was absent from home for a short period. I did not know he had been sent to prison for fraud. Things would then get back to normal. We even went on a day trip to Blackpool. But such periods of peace wouldn't last long. My dad would be back on the scene and then it wouldn't be long before the beatings would start again and with a vengeance.

Chapter Thirteen

My School Days from the Wooden Hut to our Lady of Lourdes

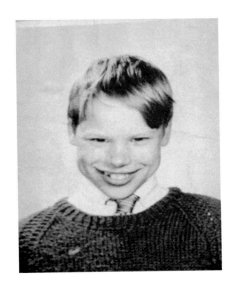

The earliest school day I can remember was when I was just four years old and the school in question was called the Wooden Hut. The year was 1962. I remember my sister Diane walking me to school from Lee street

My school uniform was miles too big for me and was probably somebody's castoffs from a neighbour in my street.

I had short grey pants and I had to use a snake belt to keep them from falling down around my ankles; a white shirt which was two sizes too big for me (at least it kept my back warm) and a pair of black shoes which were a size too big for me. I had a little shoulder bag for my lunch which consisted of an apple and few jam butties. (sandwiches)

Every Morning we used to queue outside the Lady of Lourdes church on Plodder Lane. Mrs Dillworth, my teacher at the time, then shouted out all the names on the school register When it was my turn I heard "Minihane."

"Here Miss," I replied.

"Speak louder I can't hear you," she would say.

After she finished she would march us all in military fashion into the school.

Mrs Dillworth was very strict and if you interrupted her in class she would come cover and bang her ruler hard on your school desk. She used to frighten me.

If I remember rightly our classroom was also our dinner room. There, there was a serving hatch that brought the dinner out of the kitchen.

There were only two classes and these were separated by a room divider. The school was very old and made of wood, hence the name, *The Wooden Hut.*

I wasn't long at the school. It was only a temporary measure until The Lady of Lourdes was built.

The new school opened on January 7, 1964, with 167 children on the register and six teachers. I can't remember all the names of the teachers. The ones I could remember were Mrs Dillworth who had been my teacher at the old wooden hut; Mr Cain, Mr Bunting and the head master Mr Cochran. I had the pleasure of being one of his first pupils to break a table tennis bat after he swiped my bottom for being disruptive in class.

I would feel his venom on quite a few occasions. He used different appliances like the slipper or the ruler to give me pain and he succeeded. In later years, he was ordained as a priest. I chuckled at the thought that he must have been to confession plenty of times to confess his sins before he was finally ordained a priest.

I progressed from the infants to the junior part of the school. It was here I started to get involved in sports like football and cricket. It was at a time when I was nervous of getting undressed in the changing rooms because of the bruises and marks I received from my father. These did get a bit of attention now and again and the number of times I cried on my school desk after the beatings I received from my dad didn't help but I never confided in the teachers and I kept my dad's violence a deadly secret.

I remember very well the school uniform I used to wear. White shirt with a blue and white striped tie (I always struggled to tie a knot) and I had short black pants. I would be the first to admit I was disruptive in class and very mischievous but I was just a rebellious kid.

I did get into the odd fight. One that does stand out was with a lad called Stott. We were playing five-a-side football on the school field when Stott kicked me in the ankle as I was about to score.

I retaliated and punched him in the nose so hard he fell on to the floor crying, holding his nose which was bleeding profusely. The match was abandoned and I was taken to Mr Cochran office where I was duly punished with the slipper.

I did occasionally get ten bells of shit kicked out of me and one lad called Potter did that. He was a lot bigger then me and had a dodgy eye if I remember, but it was a learning curve and we did in the end become good friends.

Even though I was suffering with abuse at home and on the odd occasion I cried on my school desk; I enjoyed my time at the school. I was even in the school choir which I found to be great fun. We were like the family unit which I missed at home.

On the educational side, I didn't do that well. I failed my eleven plus and I left the school in 1969 for another Catholic school called St Gregory's.

Chapter Fourteen

Blood, Sweat and Tears

Derwent road was a new home. It might have been new surroundings but it was the same old thing with my father. The constant beatings and his moods meant every day I was living in fear. I was constantly soiling my bed and wetting myself. I started to get large red blotches on my face which required treatment by my doctor. He told my mum it was a kind of nervous rash It was then the doctor started to ask questions to my mum about what was causing my nervous disorders She always replied that everything was fine at home. To my disgust but she was protecting the family name and she was living in fear of my dad. My father was always trying to intimidate and frighten me. He seemed to always derive pleasure from the violence.

From pushing my head under the water when I was having a bath, to nipping my side, to slapping me across my head just for the fun of it, it was constant. I always slept with the light on and if I ever heard my dad's voice I used to hide under the blankets shaking and I would frequently wet the bed. I was scared to death of him coming in and picking on me. He did this regularly. He would just come into my room and turn the light of and hold the blankets over my head until I screamed out in pain that I couldn't breathe. He would just walk out the room and laugh. I had been punched and kicked and hot cigarettes stubbed on my naked body until I begged him to stop because of the pain.

The worst kind of cruelty was when he just stared at me without saying a word for minutes on end. If I tried to walk away he would grab my hair till I screamed out in pain. If I didn't do as I was told by him he would punish me for no reason. It was all a game to him. I was his prey, a kind of sport to him and he enjoyed the suffering and pain I was going through. The only time I felt safe from him was when I was in school where I cried a thousand tears on my school desk.

Hiding under my bed was becoming more frequent or hiding in the wardrobe but my dad always found me. I could hear his voice "Ian, where are you? I'm coming to find you." This would give me constant nightmares and it still haunts me to this present day.

Events would eventually turn out even worse. It was when I was just eight years old. What happened would be the worst nightmare imaginable. It was when my father's evil intent would finally come out with a vengeance.

It was a Saturday morning and my mum was out shopping with the kids in Bolton. I was left on my own with my dad. I was playing in my bedroom with my toy soldiers. When suddenly I heard the bedroom door open. I turned around and it was my dad screaming at me, "Why are you ignoring me?"

I was shaking with fear and crying and saying, "Please don't hit me dad. I'm sorry I didn't hear you.

Then he screamed out at me again. "I wanted you to go to the shop for me but you deliberately ignored me."

Then he totally lost control and punched me. He knocked me to the floor and then knocked all my toy soldiers off the window ledge. Then he turned his attention to me. My nose was bleeding and my head was hurting. He grabbed me by the hair and dragged me across the bedroom floor as I was screaming to him please leave me alone. He pushed me onto the landing and then threw me down the stairs. I must have hit every step on the way down. I couldn't move I was in pain in my shoulder and my back. I was covered in blood. It was pouring down my face. I couldn't move and was so frightened I thought he was going to kill me. Then he left for a few minutes. I tried to get up but I was in agony. I sat against the front door shaking and crying covered in blood and wet through with my own urine and I accidentally soiled my pants. My dad then came out with a bottle which I later found out was sherry. He sat on the stairs just staring at me drinking out of the bottle. He then picked me up and pushed me against the front door. He then told me to get undressed. I couldn't do it myself, I was in pure agony. My dad just pulled the jumper over my head and I yelled out in pain. He then told me he was taking all my clothes off as I stank like a pig. He then went upstairs and got another set of clothes and a wet towel and he washed me down from top to bottom. He wiped my face clean from the blood and the soiled and wet pants and he went out and threw them in the bin.

He then told me he was taking me to the hospital and that if he told the doctors the truth he would punish me and my mum. He yelled out at me, "Do you understand Ian?"

I said, "Yes I understand. Please don't hurt me and my mummy. I won't say anything to anybody I promise."

He then telephoned for a taxi. It arrived within ten minutes. My dad put me in the taxi and he told the driver I had fallen down stairs and that I need to go to the hospital. When we arrived, my dad told me to wait and sit on a chair while he went to the front desk and not to speak to anybody. Eventually my dad came back with a nurse and a doctor and I was taken straight in to a cubicle. They asked me where the pain was. I told them in my shoulder and back and my nose and my head was aching. My dad was watching me all the time which made me feel nervous. I wanted to tell the doctor the truth but I was too frightened to do so. The doctor checked my head and said I had a small lump on my head but nothing serious. He slowly took my jumper off and felt my shoulder. I couldn't move my back as it was too painful.

He then said, "I think you have a Broken collarbone but you will need an X-ray to be sure." He then checked my back and my side and kept prodding it all over. It was very painful but he reassured me it was just badly bruised. My dad was like a changed man. He was very polite to the doctor and kept rubbing my hair as though he was concerned.

The doctor looked concerned. He asked me what happened.

I just replied, "I slipped down the stairs doctor. He just looked at me as if to say he didn't believe me but he never said anything. I was taken to the X-ray department and it was confirmed I had a broken collar bone. My shoulder was strapped up and I had to wear it for nearly 8 weeks.

When my mum came home she went crazy with my dad. "What have you done to him?"

"He fell down stairs," he replied.

She screamed at him, "I don't believe you." She took me in to the front room and asked me what happened in a tearful voice.

I lied and said, "I fell down stairs and that's the truth mum."

She kissed me on the cheek. I sobbed on her shoulder. She knew I was lying but never questioned me again, probably in fear that if she carried on questioning my dad it would make things worse.

For the next few months I felt safe. My mum kept by my side and my dad never touched me in that time but it wasn't to last long. The beatings would return and when he had enough of me he would turn his attention to my mum.

Chapter Fifteen

My Mother's tears

I don't know when the abuse started and it's not a subject that I asked her about very often. However, I'm pretty sure my dad hit her while she was pregnant with me, so it must have been in the earlier days when she first met him.

My father often had violent attacks of rage when he was drunk and angry or he had a bad day at the bookies. He was a monster and whoever stood in his way would suffer the consequences. Living in fear wasn't normal but it was the norm in our family.

My mother would always say to me, "What happens in the family stays in the family."

For the first seven years of my life, I watched my father beat up my mum. I have a vague recollection of a time when I tried to get between them, jumped in front of my mum and faced my father with every ounce of courage my tiny little body could hold, screaming at him, "Leave my Mummy alone!" I was just four years old at the time. The beatings were always behind closed doors so there were never any witnesses. To the outside world, he was a charming and educated man but he was inhuman, a sadistic and callous monster who got kicks and who would often laugh after my mother and I were beaten.

My mother often lightened our bruises with makeup, concealing them under shades of peach and beige. Whenever we had visitors she tried to hide the truth of what was going on in the house. Seared into my memory were the forceful, blunt sounds of bare knuckles colliding with my mother's face and torso. I remember the sight of ruptured blood vessels in her eyes. I recall my mother's piercing screams. I remember rounding the corner to the room where she was being assaulted. She was on the floor, lying on her back, with her hands extended upward trying to guard against the onslaught of punches from my dad standing over her. I often felt confused, betrayed, and frightened. The violence was frequent and was very violent. I did try to stop him before he would unleash another blow. And sometimes I managed to jump on his back trying to stop his blows against my mother's face but he was always too physically strong for me He was a giant towards me and was possessed.

One memory that would stand out for me long before my dad tried to strangle my mother in the hall way. I was just 8 years old and I didn't go to school on this day as I was ill. I was on my own upstairs in bed reading a comic. My father just came over and dragged me out of bed and started hitting me for no apparent reason. The Yelp of my cries alerted my mother who ran up the stairs and as always came to my rescue. A petite woman — barely over five foot five tall and maybe 130 lbs soaking wet — yet she was fearless. She yelled in his face to tell him that if he wanted to hit someone, he could hit her instead.

I sat on the floor crying as he dragged her across the landing and into their bedroom. The door closed behind them with what seemed to me, a thud of finality. This wasn't the first time he had beaten her but it wouldn't be the last. I heard her screaming, crying, desperate to escape, and I heard his almost whispered and sadistic tone as he tortured her. I felt powerless. The noise and chaos continued as the yells turned into sobs and her mutated attempts to let her go. I punched on the bedroom door and screamed for them to stop. With a burst of anger, I opened the door and told him to leave her alone. She broke free from him and started crawling towards me I remember her blue eyes meeting mine, her face streaked with tears, dirt and bruising. In contrast to hers, his dark, dead eyes met mine and he quietly said, "Close the door."

My father's larger-than-life form came up behind her, grabbed her ankle, and dragged her back in to the bedroom. I fell to the ground, feeling powerless (a feeling that lasted most of my life) and wept. I wanted to protect my mother and yet so desperately still wanted my father's approval and love, something I was never to gain. My mum's screams grew louder. I could hear pleas begging my dad to stop. It eventually did stop and my dad opened the door and laughed as he walked passed without saying a word. He went down stairs put on his coat and I heard the door shut behind him. My mother had blood on her face, on her scalp, bruises were already forming over her body, and yet, my father offered up a small scratch on his arms — defensive wounds of a small woman fighting to survive. She told me to ring for an ambulance and it wouldn't be long before the ambulance turned up at the house. She was sobbing as she looked in the mirror at her badly bruised and swollen face. She tried to talk but seemed to just mumble her words her left cheek seemed a bit distorted her mouth was crooked. I knew then she was badly hurt. She was cleaning herself up when I heard a loud bang on the door.

My mum spoke her famous words, "What happens in the family stays in the family. If they ask what happened, I fell down stairs. You listening Ian?" I opened the door and I could see the ambulance. My mum slowly came down the stairs holding the banister rail to stop her falling. The ambulance driver helped her into the ambulance and he asked my mum what happened.

She replied, "I fell down stairs."

He just looked at my mum shaking his head as if to say that he didn't believe her. We arrived at Townleys hospital which was on Minerva Road, a short ride from my house. My mum was taken straight into a cubical. I wasn't allowed in and was told to wait in the waiting room. I was crying and frightened. I was worried about my mum and I knew she would lie to the doctors about what happened. It would be a good hour before the doctor came over to me and stroked my hair and said to me your mum will be ok.

"She has had an X-ray and she has a minor fracture on her jaw. She won't be needing any surgery. She will be allowed home but must take medication for her pain."

I sobbed on the doctor's arm. He then took me to see my mum who was lying on a bed. Her face was badly swollen her eyes blood shot and her left eye was starting to blacken and swell. She held my hand and told me not to worry and not to cry as she will be fine. We went home in the ambulance. Our next-door neighbour was looking through the window. Mum just waved and tried to smile with her disjointed smile. My dad kept away till the early hours; typical of his cowardice and arrogance. It would be nearly two months before my mum's face would eventually heal and she would carry on being a mother to us all such was her strength and loving ways.

Chapter Sixteen

Auntie Ann

My auntie Ann was a lovely person who thought a lot about me and who also would become my god-parent. For whatever reason, my dad never got on with her even as a child. But I did find out later from her that he used to hit and bully her.

When I was very little I always remember her in my life. I saw more of her when I moved to Derwent Road from Lee Street. She lived on Mount Pleasant Road which wasn't very far from our house. Auntie Ann's Husband Tony was, of course, my uncle and he was sound. He always treated me well and used to buy me sweets from the corner shop. Their children Jean and Robert were my cousins and they were equally sound. Auntie Ann's house was very clean, tidy and well-furnished and had statues of Our Lady all over the house. She was very religious.

I used to stay there at the weekends and she always made me feel welcome. I used to get a lot invitations to her house to stay. I used to look forward to my Sundays as she always cooked lamb with potatoes, veg and gravy topped with mint sauce. This was a rarity in my household.

She used to take me shopping every other weekend for clothes.

Auntie Ann is the only family member I confided in about the abuse from my father. I told her everything and I cried many a time in her arms. She confronted my dad many times about it and suffered at his hands on the odd occasion and was banned for a while from coming to my house as my dad didn't like taking a few home truths.

After my Uncle Tony passed away, she got depressed and started to become dependent on prescription drugs.

She would take any form of tablet for her drug addiction from pain killers to sleeping tablets. She became such an addict that her doctor stopped giving her prescriptions. She had been going to the doctor's surgery every other day.

Many times, she would go to my mum's and beg for tablets. I Remember once my mum gave her water tablets and said they was pain killers. My auntie Ann was back the following day asking for more. She told my mum they worked wonders for her headaches. but she couldn't stop going to the toilet during the day. That must have brought a smile to my mum's face.

I felt so sorry as each day passed by her habit was getting worse. In the end my mum saw this and stopped giving her tablets and tried to help her kick the habit but she couldn't. My mum even made her appointments to see the doctor to try and get some help, but she made excuses and deliberately missed her appointments. She tried to persuade me but I couldn't do it. I loved her so much. In her desperation, she went and saw my dad and it wasn't long after that my dad banned her from coming to our house.

I remember the day well. It was after we had had our tea. I heard a knock on the front door and mum told me to go and answer it.

It was my auntie Ann. She said, "Hi Ian, I have a small treat for you." She gave me a small bar of chocolate bar which was quite usual. Even when I visited her house and stayed over she used to have a tin full of them specially for me. Anyway, she said the usual hello to the family and headed into the front room where my dad was. My mum was very concerned as my dad had had a massive argument with her over me and the beatings. I didn't know straight away but my dad used to take advantage of her and sell her tablets to feed her addiction. My dad used to get extra prescriptions so that he could sell her tablets for money to feed his own addictions. Drinking and gambling. It was a frequent arrangement they had, between them. I actually saw my dad giving her tablets. He used to put them in a brown envelope and she would just pass over money to my dad. This ended abruptly, as the doctor stopped giving my father prescriptions as he was giving the doctor all kinds of excuses to get tablets. The doctor ended it and only gave him prescriptions when he was due for a repeat. So, my auntie Ann's tablet supply came to came to an end and she had to find other ways of getting them.

I saw her coming up Derwent Road once after she been to my house, apparently, my dad had kicked her out of the house as she had no more use to him anymore. She was crying and in a bad state and told me that my dad had slapped her and banned her from the house. I was very upset and she knew it would be the very last time she ever set foot in my father's house again.

She was my god-parent and paid for all my clothes for my first communion day at Our Lady of Lourdes and was even there to support me but sadly she was at the back of the church. My father disowned her and wouldn't speak to her.

I still visited her at her house but this would be on the odd occasion as I went my own way and did different things. She sadly died several years later after I had moved away from home. It wasn't the tablets that killed her but old age. She was a lovely person and very caring, my auntie Anne. She stood up for me against my father but she struggled in life after my uncle Tony died which made her very depressed and it was that that caused her addiction to prescription drugs.

My dad treated her very badly for his own reasons instead of helping her when she needed it the most. This was something I would remind him about in my older years. He turned his back on her when she needed him the most.

R.I.P Auntie Anne. You will always be sadly missed and always in my thoughts.

Chapter Seventeen

Communion Day 1966

I was never really a practicing catholic boy or even a good one. The only time I enjoyed going to church was at Christmas and Easter when I used to get gifts and an Easter egg. I always made a special effort to go then. My family wasn't really religious although my brother Mark was a practising altar boy and had plans to be a priest when he was older, but that soon fell by the wayside. As for my parents, my mum always wore a gold cross and chain but it was more of a gesture than anything else.

My dad was a total hypocrite, he made us pray to God at every mealtime thanking him for putting the food on the table. I do remember in my naive innocence asking God to protect me against my father; of course, this never happened.

I wasn't a disbeliever I just couldn't understand the catholic religion. If there was ever a God, how come he let my dad beat me and my mum? And if my dad was a Christian how come he did such evil things to my family. I was totally confused. The only time I ever saw my dad go to church was at Christmas. Then he would go in to the Lourdes club for a drink. Yet he forced the family to go every Sunday. The only time I can ever remember my dad giving me any money was for the church collection. I pretended to put the money in when the money tray passed along the pews. I spent the money in the corner shop on sweets and pop. I thanked God for his generosity. I started to skip church and would hide in the dell and just lay on the grass. I used to wave to my mum on her way to the church and then meet up with her after it finished.

The school I went to was a catholic school. It was called our lady of Lourdes. They practised the religion seriously and I had to go to classes for my confirmation. Confirmation, a sacrament of initiation, establishes young adults as a fully -fledged members of the faith. This sacrament was called Confirmation because faith given in Baptism was now confirmed and made strong.

During your baptism, your parents and God-parents make promises to renounce Satan and believe in God and the church on behalf of the child. During confirmation, the focus is on the Holy Spirit who confirmed the Apostles on Pentecost and gave them courage to practice their faith. Catholics believe that the same Holy Spirit confirms Catholics during the sacrament of confirmation and gives the same gifts.

You had to confess your sins by going to confession to cleanse your soul of the sins before you had your first communion. I remember that day very well. I was very nervous. I had to go into a side room in the church. Then I had to kneel on the bench in front of a small window-like opening with a fine wire mesh over it. I think the idea was I couldn't see the priest but I could hear him. I was already informed beforehand what to expect from the priest and what to say. I couldn't remember who spoke first but I do remember saying, "forgive me father I have sinned. I knocked a policeman's helmet off."

I swear I heard a slight chuckle followed by, "I want you to ask forgiveness and say three Hail Marys."

On my Communion day, I was up very early. I was slightly nervous as it was the biggest event on the Catholic calendar. My mum had been saving up hard for this special day along with my Auntie Ann who was my god-parent. They put the money together and they bought me a white shirt and tie and black pants and a pair of shiny black shoes. The whole family, including my dad, turned out for this special day. The church was full to the rafters. All the boys from my school were there wearing similar clothes. As for the girls, they all wore white dresses with white head veils. During the Mass, we had to queue up in front of the priest for our bread and wine. I remember accidentally biting the priest's finger. He yelled out in pain but then he blessed me and I went back to the bench giggling. After the Mass, we all walked around the estates near the church with all the school banners and a small band playing some music. I must admit I felt like royalty as all the roadside was packed with families and friends. My mum made me feel like a million dollars. I still have the communion medal (Saint Christopher) my Auntie Ann bought me and the certificate for the first communion my school gave me.

My dad shook my hand on this day and held me close. This was the only time, other than Christmas Day, that he ever did that. As for my mum, she couldn't stop smiling at me, she was so happy and so proud. It was a godsend for me to see her so happy after all the pain she was suffering at the hands of my father.

Chapter Eighteen

The Window of Tears

One day that will always stay in my mind and would affect my life for ever and be my worst nightmare imaginable.

I was just nine years old. I got up late as usual and got the usual evil eyes and moans from my father. When I sat at the breakfast table, I rushed eating my toast and jam and the cup of tea my mum had made. It was not too sweet and milky and was just the way I liked it but I didn't get the chance to drink it. My father knocked the cup over purposely and it splashed across my face, onto my blue school jumper and my black short pants. My father laughed as I screamed out in pain as it burned my face and bare legs. He turned to my mum with his demonic eyes to say leave him or you will get the same. But she ignored his evil intentions and wiped my face and legs with her pinny and held me tightly to calm me down.

My father strutted out of the front room and he shouted, "Bitch you fucking bitch. You're too soft with him."

My mum ignored his remarks and just tried to calm me down by stroking my blonde locks. I sobbed so much my eyes started to hurt. I was shaking with fear. My mum undressed and changed me and put another jumper on and pants.

Mum left the room for a second to get my coat and then she grabbed my hand and said, "I'm taking you to school. Come along, Ian you are late."

I didn't want to go to school. I was a mess. I was shaking and crying all the way. My mum tried her best to calm me down. She left me at the school gates and she gave me a kiss and then waved me off. The day at school was a long one. I cried on my desk a few times and this would happen on a regular basis.

The school bell rang it was time to leave. School time had finished. I collected my school bag and belongings and headed towards the school gates. I decided to go the long way around and took my time walking home.

I just couldn't face being in that house any more. I walked up Plodder Lane and cut through the dell and lay on the grass for a while. I then sat on a grass banking and I started to shake. I was very fearful about facing my father. I started to sob. I just wanted my life to end. I couldn't take it anymore. I was fed up with all the arguments, the beatings and seeing my mother crying and listening to her screams throughout the night when my dad came home drunk and did whatever he felt like doing.

I climbed over the fence and headed past the coal yard on Highfield Road and headed home slowly. I was already late, nearly an hour in total. I walked past the shops at the top of Derwent Road and I could see my house in the distance. I stated to shake with fear. I wet myself and my short school pants were wet through. I could feel the urine running down my leg and in to my shoe. I slowly walked down Derwent road. Instead of knocking on the front door I decided to go around to the back of the house and peep through the kitchen or the back-room window to see if I could see my mum and to wait for a signal that it was safe to enter the house. I crept around the back and I could hear screams. I looked through the kitchen window and in the hallway, I saw my mother being dragged by her hair across the floor with the odd boot going in on my mum's body on the floor. I screamed through the window to leave my mother alone I was crying my heart out. My father grabbed my mother off the floor by her hair and shoved her against the front door.

Her screams torment me to this very day. I was banging hard on the window so hard, I didn't realise my knuckles were swollen, such was the impact on the window. My father was oblivious to my screams and the constant banging on the window. I ran up Derwent Road screaming and crying. I headed for the phone box facing the cooperative shop. I saw one of my neighbours Mrs Holiday who was already in the phone box. I banged the phone box door and screamed at her to call the police as my father was beating my mother in the hallway. She put the phone down and called the police. She then told me the police were on their way. I ran like a bat out of hell down Derwent Road and headed for the kitchen window. I could still hear my mum screaming and crying. Then I saw he had his hands on her throat. He was trying to strangle her.

I was screaming, "Please leave her alone." I was petrified. Then suddenly it all stopped. My father ran in to the front room and I could see my mum opening the front door and two large men with helmets on, in black uniform came in. It was the police. I felt safe now so I ran around to the front door. It was wide open and there I saw my father on his hands and knees begging my mother and crying not to let the police take him away. I knew he was lying but I was too afraid to say anything. I didn't want to face my father later if she let him off the hook.

The police wanted to take my father away and lock him up for good. I prayed to God that they would take him away and throw the key away. But to my shock she told the burly police officers, that she wouldn't press any charges against him and to their disgust she told them she would give him one more chance. The police offices begged my mum to change her mind as my father would do it again.

She repeated again, "I will give him one more chance and if he ever does it again, I will definitely get him locked up for good. If he ever lays a hand on me, that will be that."

The police left and my father just put his coat on and left without saying a word. He banged the door behind him and probably headed to the Flying Shuttle, the local pub for his usual drinking bout with his friends. They all thought butter wouldn't melt in his mouth. Little did they know what went on behind closed doors. My father was a Jekyll and Hyde character and a coward who bullied women and young children.

I looked at my mother she was shaking on the stairs crying her eyes out. She was a complete nervous wreck. Her hair was a mess and her face looked tormented. Her eyes were all puffed up and her left eye was swelling up and would eventually turn black. Her bottom lip was bleeding and probably needed stitching. I muttered to my mother and said why didn't you get him locked up for good and then the beatings would stop.

She replied that if he went to prison who would put food on the table, "Who would pay the rent? We could lose the house and end up in cottage homes for the homeless. I don't want my family in a place like that. Please understand Ian I have to do this my way and keep my family together."

I sat on my mum's knee and I cried forgetting that I was wet through with my urine. She went upstairs and cleaned us both up. I saw her look in the mirror at her face. I could see tears running down her face. She then put on some makeup to cover her swelling eyes which were blackening up by the minute. Then she brushed her hair and turned around and said, "Time for tea Ian," with a broken smile, as though nothing had happened.

When we went downstairs she said, "Come along Ian, you can help me cut up the potatoes."

She had the chance to end all the beatings and the mental abuse once and for all but such was the women's bravery she carried on for the sake of the family and the suffering would carry on for a little while longer.

Chapter Nineteen

The Ice-Cream Wars

Farnworth was well-known for having characters good and bad. Antonio was no different. He was Italian and an ice-cream man and he always played the Mr Softee tune or jingle when we saw him in our street, to let everybody know he was there. He was well known as Mr Whippy around Highfield. He was only small about 5ft 7 with short black curly hair and was quite tubby. He had a round tubby face with dark eyes and a small moustache and he spoke with a soft Italian accent. Antonio was always smiling he used to call me cheeky chops because I never had the right amount of money to buy an ice cream. Whenever I tried to buy an ice-cream, I used to show Antonio what money I had in my hand and give him one of my cheeky smiles. I always asked for a 99 cornet which was an ice cream with a flake in the middle knowing too well I didn't have enough money. Antonio just shook his head and smiled. I usually got a broken cornet with a bit of whipped iced-cream.

I always said to him, "Is that all?"

Antonio used to just laugh and wink at me and say, "On your way before I take it back from you."

Antonio knew me and my friends by our first names and whenever we heard the ice cream jingle I used to run to my mum and beg for some money which more than often I didn't get.

So, Mick, Frank and I used to wait on the corner of our street and queue up in anticipation.

When it was my turn Antonio would say to me, "What are you having cheeky chops?"

I always replied with a sad face which usually worked with my mum, if I wanted anything or had done anything wrong, so I used the same trick with Antonio and said I had no money that day.

Antonio would lean over and rub my hair and with a big smile say, "Here you are cheeky chops."

He would give me a couple of broken cornets with a bit of ice-cream and strawberry sauce on top. I would just thank him and run off with my friends with a big smile on my face.

Mick and Frank used to always share their ice cream with me. That's when you knew what real friends were, when I was short. If I had money, we used to spend it on each other. We might have been poor but we always looked after each other.

One week a different ice cream man came into our street, he was called Manfredi. He was also Italian but completely different to Antonio. He was tall with a bald head and very well built and not as friendly. I tried the same tricks I used with Antonio but Manfredi wasn't as polite or as generous. He would just tell me to bugger off if I didn't have any money, or go and ask my parents for some money. I used to walk away with tears rolling down my face. Mick and Frank as usual always had money from their parents and they would always break a bit of cornet off with a bit of ice cream on. This used to always cheer me up. They both knew I was going through a bad time with my dad and that's why they were very protective of me.

The same ice-cream man turned up again and I tried the same trick. "Do you have any broken cornets?" I said to him.

He just replied, "Bugger off if you have no money just don't come to my ice-cream van again. You are banned."

I missed Antonio and the banter I had with him. He was always friendly and he always put a smile on my face.

I remember once Antonio saw me with a large bruise on my left cheek and he asked me how had I got it.

"I just replied that I fell over." Antonio got out of the ice-cream van and gave me a cuddle and started to get upset.

"I don't believe you," he replied. "Did your parents hit you?"

I said, "No, honestly. I fell."

He just replied that if they ever touched me I must tell him.

Antonio wasn't the first person to ask me. I would always give the same answer that I fell.

I never saw Antonio for weeks but one day I was playing football in my street with Frank when I saw the Antonio ice-cream van park at the bottom of my street. I was so happy. Mick and I cheered and ran to the ice-cream van but within seconds, we saw Manfredi pull up at the side of him.

The Manfredi guy got out of his van and started shouting in Italian at Antonio. The arguing was loud and vicious and I must admit, I was frightened. I just wanted to run away but I was frozen to the spot. Antonio got out of his ice cream-van and started to wag his finger at the Manfredi guy. It wasn't long before they both came to blows and Antonio got the better of the Manfredi guy. He punched him twice and knocked him to the ground. All the bawling and shouting got most of the residents out of their houses in our street, such was the noise.

It wasn't long before the cavalry arrived. It was Sergeant Swann, our local police officer. I was happy to see him which was a first for me. He separated them and gave them what appeared to be a serious telling off. We all started to cheer when the blooded Manfredi guy jumped into his ice cream van and drove out of the street. That was the last time I ever saw him.

Antonio cleaned himself up and then he played his jingle tone again so we all formed a queue. Sergeant Swann was first in the queue and Antonio gave him a double 99 ice-cream cornet and told him it was on the house and then thanked him. Mick and I along with Frank got the same as Sergeant Swann, a double 99 ice cream cornet with a chocolate flake with all the trimmings and free of charge.

Antonio carried on selling ice-cream for several more years until he died. That was a sad day for all of us. Antonio will always be a special part of my life. R.I.P Antonio.

Even to this day when I every hear the ice-cream jingle to the tune of Mr Softee, I always think of Antonio.

Chapter Twenty

Little Nanny

During the early seventies, my father's mother came to live with us, for a while. We used to call her Little Nanny for obvious reasons, she was very small just like my dad.

She was a lovely person. She had both legs amputated because of gangrene that she had caught on one leg but spread to her other leg. She was a lovely person, completely different from my dad. Every Friday, without fail, she used to give me sixpence along with my other two brothers and my sister Pat. It was sort of a treat and she really enjoyed seeing us all with a smile on our faces.

My sisters Denise and Diane, had already moved on to pastures new. Diane had moved to Leicester and Denise moved to Brixham near Torquay.

My brother who had Epileptic fits caused by the meningitis on his brain when he was a young child, had also moved to a special home on Moss Bank Road in Bolton, as he needed 24 hour caring with special nurses.

My sister moved into the box-room to my annoyance, as I wanted the room for myself. So, I still stayed in the same room with my other two brothers.

My father used to wait for me behind the front room door when he knew little nanny had given me a treat. As soon as I left the room he used to grab it and take it from me for no reason. He just laughed and said I'll make better use of it (no doubt for his drinking and gambling habits.) I was heartbroken as he only ever took it from me not the others. I used to sob on the stairs when my brothers and sisters came back home from the shops on Highfield after they spent their treats on the penny tray (mixture of different toffees.) I was heartbroken. I really did hate my dad for the way he treated me.

My Little Nanny, like I said, was only small with short grey hair and she wore spectacles. She had a wheelchair in which, now and again, I used to push her around the estate or to the shops and she used to treat me for taking her out. Maybe she got wind of what my father was like and this was her way off making sure I was treated. My Little Nanny slept downstairs in a single bed and my mum used to look after her by washing her down and cleaning the dressings for her legs, as well as cooking and cleaning and going to work. My mum was so tired. I used to see her fast asleep on the couch in the back room, absolutely exhausted.

I used to love my little chats with my Little Nanny. We always talked about the old days. I used to sit next to her for hours talking about the First World War and one tale that she told me was she once saw a giant Zeppelin in the sky above her house where she lived in Bolton. A German Zeppelin was a large cylindrical rigid airship, built from 1900 to carry passengers and in World War I for bombing and reconnaissance. She also talked about the old ammunition factory that she worked in and the long hours and how dangerous it was. She loved talking about the old communities and how difficult it was to live in the old times.

She used to make me laugh. "We didn't have televisions then I tell thee or washing machines. We used to wash our clothes in the sink and drain them out with our bare hands. It was tough in them days.

She mentioned my dad a few times saying, he was very quiet when he was a baby but she didn't talk in too much detail.

Her favourite was Margaret, my dad's sister, she told me, When I was little she used to take me for long walks in the pram around Farnworth. She also told me that Margaret had a baby shop called *Tots* on Market Street in Farnworth and always dressed me in the best baby clothes when I was a baby. I know this was true, as my mum told me the same.

She also talked about my Auntie Anne, my dad's sister and she told me she was a kind and a generous person but she never got on with my dad as they were always fighting and arguing, when they were kids. She was a very gentle person and was kind and caring the complete opposite to my father.

One day when I came home after school I heard my mum arguing with my dad. I was standing at the front door when my dad came out. When he saw me he just pushed me to the floor, for no reason. I watched him walking up the road staggering, he was obviously drunk and heading to the Flying Shuttle pub for another round of drinks.

I went inside and I saw my mum picking up my Little Nanny up from the floor. My dad had apparently lost his temper and turned the wheelchair over because my Little Nanny refused to give him any money for beer knowing too well what he would be like, after a drink.

It would be later that I found out that he used to hit his own mother on a regular occasion if he didn't get his own way or if he needed money for a drink; times never change.

My Little Nanny I know, used to tell my dad off on many occasions for his cruelty towards my mum but he completely ignored her.

In the end, it got too difficult for mum to look after her as well as looking after the family and the house. She ended up in a Convalescent home with specialist nurses who would have the time and caring she needed. Deep down I thought my mum did it to protect my Little Nanny from my dad's violent ways.

For whatever reason my little nanny died not long after she left Derwent Road. Apparently, she died of natural causes. I always said she died of a broken heart.

On the morning of my Little Nannies funeral, for whatever reason, my dad took his grief out on me. I think I was 13 years old at the time. I just came into the front room to ask my mum if my black tie looked okay? I always struggled to tie it in a knot. My dad came straight at me and punched me in the face and repeatedly until my mum separated us, then he just walked out the room, without saying a word. My left eye was badly swollen and my nose was bleeding and it ran down onto my white shirt. I was so upset and angry and I am to this day. I never knew why he attacked me. My mum always said it was guilt after the way he treated his own mother and I happened to be the punch bag that he would take it out on.

It was a hot summer's day and I remember it because of Wimbledon. At the funeral, he never spoke a word to me. I remember my dad at the graveside but I don't ever remember him losing any tears.

Little Nanny was a lovely kind and caring person. My dad definitely didn't deserve her as his mother. I will always remember her with kind thoughts and the lovely little chats we had together.

R.I.P Little Nanny, I miss you a lot.

Chapter Twenty-One

Drinking on Piggy

At the age of nine I stole a bottle of cider from the co-operative corner shop at the top of Derwent Road where I lived. Drinking was becoming a problem for me and was getting out of control and I didn't realise it at the time. My life was becoming unbearable. Drinking and getting into mischief was the only way I could cope with the constant beatings I was getting from my father and watching my mother suffering.

Whenever I was let out I used to get together with a few of my friends. I won't mention the names for obvious reasons. Let's just say there were a few of us. Mick, Liam, Stan and Smithy, all from Highfield where I lived. We were always getting into mischief, causing havoc with the locals by fighting at football matches following our beloved Bolton Wanderers. We became close friends right through our youth.

Any time I ever got out of the house we used to meet up at the shops at the top of Derwent Road. The first thing we did was to enter the co-operative shop and pretend we were buying something. Smithy would stay outside the shop and keep an eye out for the infamous Sergeant Swann. Mick would chat to the lady at the till to distract her. She was quite a big lady who was in her early 50s. Her name was June. I used to call her fatty June. She used to speak to my mum whenever they met in the street or in the shop. While Mick was talking to fatty June, me and Stan and Liam would shove bottles of cider under our coats and jumpers and just walk out. We would then head to a place called 'Piggy' which was a small woodland and fields surround by a small lodge.

There, we had a little den, it was made of wooden planks and bits of wood which we collected from a small building site. Inside the wooden den there were blankets which I had smuggled out of my house. It was very cosy and it kept us warm and dry from the inclement weather and prying eyes.

The drinking session only lasted for about three hours as I had to be back in my house for 8pm. Nevertheless, we drank four bottles of cider, between us. I started to feel unwell. I started to vomit profusely. I tried to get up but I fell over. Mick started to panic he started to shake me and kept repeating you look ill. After about 40 mins I started to come around. I couldn't remember anything. There was only Mick and Stan who stayed behind to look after me. The rest had disappeared. It was now 9.25 and I should have been home for 8 o'clock. I started to panic. I knew I was in serious trouble so I headed back home. I vomited all the way home. I arrived at my house nearly two hours late. It was nearly 10 o' clock. I knocked on the front door hoping and praying it would be my mum who answered it. But to my shock it was my father.

He screamed at the top of his voice, "Where have you been?"

Before I could get a word in edge ways he dragged me by my hair through the front door and started to hit me in the face. I was screaming at the top of my voice telling him I was sorry but he just carried on hitting me all over my body. It was only the intervention of my mum that stopped the beating getting any worst. My dad disappeared into the front room and I started to cry in my mum's arms. I was shaking with fear. I started to vomit again so my mum took me upstairs to the bath room. She wiped all the blood from my face and started to undress me. I was covered in blood and my body was bruised all over. My mum asked me if I had been drinking and I told her that I had. My mum just shook her head in disgust and started to cry which made me feel worse. I told my mum I was sorry and that it wouldn't happen again but of course I lied and it did. She washed me down and wiped all the blood off and put me in my pyjamas, she then kissed me on my left cheek and put me in to my bed. I looked around and my sister Pat and my brother Mark were fast asleep. I remember I didn't sleep too much that night as I was sore all over. I was banned from going out with my friends for two weeks. My mum took me to school and my mum picked me up after school. After I had my tea, I went straight to bed and this carried on for the whole two weeks.

After the ban, I was let out but I had to be back in for 7pm. I met up with my usual friends at the shops on Highfield. We couldn't go in the co-operative for any cider as my mum had put a stop to it. She had spoken with fatty June who had politely banned us all from entering the premises.

Stealing cider and beer from the shops was getting harder and harder so we started to travel further afield. I got caught by Sergeant Swann pinching some bottles of beer from Flanagan's paper shop. As usual I got a thick ear from him and a good pasting from my dad when he found out.

The beatings didn't stop and my drinking seemed to be getting worse. I didn't particularly like alcohol but the effect it had on me made me happy. In a way, it helped me to forget the suffering and the pain. I knew my mum was upset and it was wrong, what I was doing but I couldn't help myself or stop myself heading down the slippery path of self-destruction.

Chapter Twenty-Two

Crying for Freedom

My father's moods changed on a regular basis. If he had been drinking or gambling he would become very manipulative towards me, today you would call it mental torture. He would slap me across the head or nip my arms or parts of my body whenever he passed me by. I always seemed to have permanent bruises on my body. He would always smile behind his demonised eyes which seemed to look straight through me and send a shiver down my spine. He had no compassion if he hurt me or not, it was just a game for him at times, I was the prey and he was the huntsman. I was his trophy. He would always bait me hoping that I would retaliate and say something back to him or hit him back and if I did find the ultimate courage, his punishment would be twice as severe. He would always put his head in my face and say I'm a coward and that I am no son of his. I always felt, since I could remember, that I wasn't good enough for him.

Turning to drink at a very young age was a like pain killer for me. I didn't particularly like the taste of drink but I liked the after-effects of being drunk to forget everything. I enjoyed the excitement of stealing bottles of cider from the co-operative shops, it was a challenge and I liked the danger of trying not to be caught but I was on numerous occasions by Sergeant Swann.

I liked the comraderie of my friends. I just wanted to be accepted and loved.

After the drinking escapades and stealing at the local shops to feed my cravings and the police getting involved, my father had had enough of me and the only way he could put a stop to it all was to keep me in my room, to keep me out of mischief. The only time I saw my friends was at school. Mick and Frank went to different schools so they used to meet at the corner shop every morning. We would carry on knocking off bottles of cider and it was at this time that I started smoking. I coughed so much that it made me sick. Frank laughed his socks off as he thought it was funny.

We all used to head off to an old run-down house on the flower estate which wasn't far from my house but away from prying eyes. Drinking and smoking were new for me but were becoming another bad habit and another craving. It would come to an end soon, when one of our neighbours caught us all drunk staggering on Plodder Lane one afternoon.

I didn't know any of this till I got home. As soon as my dad saw me at the window he opened the door and dragged me in. He went into a mad frenzy and he punched me all over my body until I was knocked unconscious. I woke up naked in my bed and I saw my mum sitting on the corner of my bed stroking my hair and sobbing. She told me she undressed me and washed me down because I was covered in blood and vomit. She leant over and held me in her arms. I just broke down crying.

I kept repeating myself, "I'm sorry mum but I can't take any more pain. I'm hurting all over. Nearly every day he hurts me, why does he not love me? He's my dad I sighed." I sobbed on my mum's shoulder while she held me tight.

She pushed my head up and said, "Ian, you must stop drinking and getting in to mischief. You are breaking my heart and it makes your dad worse. You must stop it all now before you are taken away from us and put in a home."

As tears started to roll down my cheeks I made a promise to my mum that I would behave and stop drinking, which I knew I couldn't keep. I knew I was hurting my mother but I couldn't stop, I was getting out of control. I just couldn't handle the hatred and the constant beatings from my father. I just wanted him to love me and I just couldn't understand why he hated me so much.

My mum dealt me a blow and just came straight out with it, "Ian, from now on, till you prove you can behave and change your ways, I will be walking you to school and picking you up every day. After your tea and at the weekends you will have to stay in your room."

My mum as usual kept to her word. I put up with it for a few weeks until I got bored and fed up looking at the four square walls, so one night I decided enough was enough. I crept out of my room across the landing into the box-room, opened the window and jumped onto the window ledge. Then I crawled down the drain pipe and ran like a bat out of hell to the shops to look for Mick and Frank. I would stay out for an hour then sneak back into the house, up the drain pipe through the window and into my bedroom, as though nothing happened. Of course, I only got away with it for so long. My mum found out and caught me at the shops playing football with Frank. She would just drag me home with a ticking off and put me back in to my room. The cat and mouse games would carry on for a few more weeks until my dad put his foot down by putting a lock on my bedroom door. I was allowed to come down for my tea and watch TV for a while then off I was back into my cell which I used to sarcastically say to my mum hoping she would let me out.

My mum did make things easier she bought me toy soldiers and army tanks to play with which I did most nights and now and again she bought me a model kit of a Spanish galleon or a German battleship. I used to build them from scratch and paint them and this became a hobby of mine and it certainly made my mum very happy as I was keeping out of mischief and of course, drinking.

After a few months of being locked in to my room, I was allowed out a couple of nights a week for an hour to see if I behaved. Of course, it didn't take me long to get back into the routine of getting into mischief. Then, it was back into my cell, locked away for weeks on end and this carried on right through to my early teens and I was feeling more rebellious by the day.

Chapter Twenty-Three

St Gregory's

Author on front row, third from right

No matter who you are, what you do, how old you get, your memories from school will always remain among your prized memories. Your days at school - the times when you and your friends sat on the last bench and ate your tiffin during class; the times when your best friend 'helped' you with the answers to a test and all you had to do in return was buy him an ice cream; the detentions that gave you some of your best friends; the first taste of rebellion you got from bunking a class; the first crushes; the first heartbreaks; the most wonderful memories from the best time of your life. Well this is my story of my time at St. Gregory's.

It was August 1969, I remember my first school day well. I was late getting up as usual and the only reason I got up was when I heard my dad's angry voice telling me to get up now, or I was going to get a thick ear.

I quickly put on my school uniform for my new school for the first time. Green jumper, long black pants with a white shirt and green and white tie, as usual I struggled fixing my tie. My palms were sweaty, my legs were sore, and my arms were heavy. Fear started taking over. The thought of going to a new school petrified me. I was afraid how I would do.

My mum tried her best to calm me down she walked me up Derwent Road and left me at the shops. I watched her as she waved me goodbye. I was on my own now. I started to walk down Highfield Road and in the distance, I could see St Gregory's school. I took a deep breath and headed for the school entrance. I nearly peed in my pants when I saw a group of lads who were much older and bigger then me running towards me. I was caught and pushed head first into a school bin. This was an initiation test for all newcomers. This carried on for a few days I was getting scared and came to the point where I didn't want to go to school any more. That decision would soon be taken out of my hands. Matters got worst on my third day at school. A lad in the third year approached me. He was much bigger and looked stronger than me. He tried to put me in the school bin. I don't know if it was because I was nervous or afraid but I hit him in the face and knocked him over the school bin. He ran off crying and ran to a school teacher. It was Mr Eckersley, the deputy head of the school who become my adversary in time. He grabbed my ear and dragged me into his office which would become like my second home. I got a good telling off. He wouldn't listen to me, such was his arrogance. I was told I was staying behind on detention for thirty minutes to do 500 lines. This punishment usually increased the more you got into trouble. He threatened if it happened again, he would write a letter to my parents, which sent a shiver down my spine, knowing it would result in to another good hiding from my dad. After I finished my lines, I knocked on Eckersley's door and was told to come in.

I handed him the sheet and then with a smirk on his face he told me, "See you soon." As I was walking out of the school gates I was approached by the lad I had hit earlier, but this time he wasn't on his own. He had four older lads with him, for back up. My first intention was to run but they all attacked me like a pack of animals. I was punched to the ground and kicked all over my body. I crawled into a ball to protect my face. I was screaming out and begging them to stop. It was only the intervention of an old lady shouting at them if they didn't stop she would call the police. That stopped me getting a severe beating. I thanked the old lady and staggered away. I was a mess. My face was covered in blood I was aching all over after the punishment I had received. My brand-new school jumper was ripped and as I got closer to my house reality then sunk in. I wasn't just late home from school but I had been fighting at school. I knew my dad would be angry with me. After all it was my first week in my school. Even if I was innocent I would still feel his wrath. Luckily for me my dad wasn't in.

My mum answered the door took me straight up stairs and washed all the blood off my face. She didn't say much. I just told her I was being picked on. I made sure I ate my tea upstairs to avoid my dad. I didn't see him until the morning when I was having my breakfast. He saw my face and he angrily hit me across my face and called me a coward for not standing up to them. It was obvious my mum had told him. But he never listened to reason if I didn't get a black eye at school, I would get one from him whenever it suited him to do so.

I decided enough was enough. I was sick of getting bullied by my dad and at school. I started to skip off school on a regular basis in my first year. I would hide in the building on Derwent Road all day. I went into Bolton and walked round the shops. I even hid in the coal bunker now and again; anything to skip school.

This went on for months, then ganger, Mr Greenhalgh, the headmaster, wrote a letter to my mum and dad about the absenteeism from school and if it carried on I could be expelled from school.

After a good lecture from my mum and the usual beating from my dad, I thought it would be wiser to go back school. School meals were always free for me as my dad wasn't working and there wasn't much money coming into our household. I was stigmatised in my class for it and I was always being called a peasant and laughed at in class.

The first year soon passed. I was still rebellious and getting in to mischief.

I was now in the second year and getting used to all the teachers. I always got a clip round my head, for being cheeky to him, from Mr Eckersley who was a pain in the backside.

My class teacher was Mr Southern. I got on pretty well with him, until one day in one of our science/physics lessons I recall blowing up a Liebig's condenser in style. There must have been a tiny flaw in the Pyrex because it shattered all over the room and part of it catapulted right across the lab.

We had very little opportunity to 'play' with Bunsen burners in our Science classes, as they mainly revolved around Physics. The only time I recall using the Bunsen

Burner was when we were studying the Coefficient of Linear Expansion of Metals. However, one experiment I performed in my own time was an attempt to make wine. I'd collected a load of blackberries and stuffed them into a pint-sized pop bottle with the old screw-in solid stopper. Along with the blackberries I'd also put some sugar and a little water too then hid the concoction behind a radiator in the classroom.

During the following term, it would have been January or February, when the school heating was in full flow the bottle burst during one of our lessons and it sent a bright purple plume up the classroom wall and onto the ceiling. For weeks afterwards, there was a heady smell of wine in that room - and they never did discover who the culprit was! But they did have their suspicions. I would have owned up but the headmaster, and some of the teachers, gave me the impression that they took exception to innovative people.

Mr Walsh was my favourite teacher. He was always helpful in class. I got on really well with him, plus the fact history was my favourite subject. I always got top grades. He did catch me once with a few others jumping off the bus on our school sports day after cheating in one of our mini marathons. A few others and I had to apologise to the whole school in our school assembly in the main hall.

It was only the year before I was in the main hall collecting a school prize, a book called Treasure Island by Robert Stevenson. That was for not having a day off in my second year and that was only because the school bus took me to school after my first-year escapades of skipping school.

Mr Taylor was my maths teacher. I didn't get on to well with him as I hated maths. I couldn't reckon up for toffee. If I interrupted the class I would face his wrath. Now and again he would throw the board duster at me, which hurt I can tell thee.

My English teacher was Mrs Briggs. I liked her as a person and that's probably the only reason why I liked English lessons even though I couldn't read or spell very well. She was always very helpful in class.

My brother Mark and I became the school joke because of our haircuts. They used to call us the Beatles because we had the same haircuts. My mum used to cut our hair by putting a pudding basin on our head and cutting round it - thanks mum.

My sister Pat got on very well in school and was much loved. All the boys used to fancy her. My youngest brother Stephen also came to the school but I had already left.

The first few years seemed to pass very quickly. The bullying had come to an end as I had started to fight back. I lost count of the number of fights I had on the school yard or on Dixon Green. I lost a few but some I won. I started to gain respect from the school lads. I still had trouble with the infamous Mr Eckersley. I was fighting on the school yard when Eckersley came over. He hit me so hard across the face that the impact knocked me flying over the bin. I remember running to the toilet where I locked myself in one of the toilet cubicles sobbing. My face was badly swollen and I carried on crying in the class-room.

Because of his actions, my mum and dad came into school the following day to see him and apparently, my dad knocked him over his school desk. He never hit me again after that. We still crossed paths and I lost count the number of time I received the strap and the cane from him. He used to save me till the very last, until he had dealt with all the other offenders and he always had a big grin on his face when I got punished by him. I was never away from his office. I didn't need to knock on his door. He would say, "Come in Ian I have been expecting you." I did get my little revenges on him. I used to put drawing pins on his chair. On one occasion, I threw a stink-bomb through his office window and called him a wanker, as I ran off. When I did eventually meet up with him, he hit me so hard with the cane on my bottom, I couldn't sit down for days such was the pain but it was well worth it.

Eckersley used to have his own trade-mark; he used to have studs on his shoes. You could hear him a mile off walking down the school corridors. Everybody used to stand to his attention when he walked past but I never did, to his annoyance.

I still wasn't settled at home. I was still being beaten by my father. I started to struggle in classes and my school reports were suffering. As a result, the headmaster wrote a letter to my mother stating his concerns. I was starting to be more rebellious and I was getting into more fights and generally causing mischief.

I didn't bother too much with the girls. I did have a few cuddles now and again behind the bike sheds. But it was getting into fights which was more fun. We started to fight other schools like Harper Green and George Toms. They were never any match for us, such was the hardcore of lads we had at our school.

Our main rivals on this front were St James, just up the road from our school. Now and again they would be brave and meet us outside the school gates without any warning. They would ambush us all, walking out in small groups. I had a one-to-one with one of them. He was one of the cocks of his year. I totally embarrassed him in the middle of the road, completely oblivious to the fact that we both stopped the traffic.

St James got the better of us at the beginning but we soon put that to bed. All the years from our school decided to teach St James a lesson that they would never forget. There were a good 150 lads from our school all armed to the teeth with sticks and all kinds of weapons. We all walked up to St James and waited on the top of the road where they all had to walk. Then we all charged down the hill and chased them back into school a few ran through the estates. They all ran for their lives. Quite a few of them did get a serious kicking and there were rumours that a couple of teachers were caught in the melee. We heard the police sirens and it was time to flee. I got chased through Newbury for what seemed like hours but I got away. Some didn't and were punished accordingly the following day, with the strap.

I used to dread my reports and taking them home as I knew my dad would be angry. He always told me I was thick as a barge-poll followed by a crack round my head.

The latter years at school were more enjoyable. In the fourth year, we had our own new building separate from the rest for the fourth and fifth formers. We had our own restaurant and we had our own smoke room for the smokers.

There used to be a pub called the Grapes near Dixon Green. Now and again, we would go for a couple of beers in the school dinner-time. It wouldn't take much for me to get drunk; two beers and I was well gone. I fell asleep on the bowling green. I was so drunk that I missed all the afternoon lessons.

Every Christmas the school had a party it was strictly no alcohol, but we used to smuggle drinks in and spike some of the girls' drinks which came in handy at the end of the night when it was time for our Christmas kisses as they were slightly intoxicated. I was drunk out of my mind and had to be carried home. I was really out of it. I couldn't remember if my dad beat me or not which was a good thing.

I still skipped school now and again. On one occasion, me and a couple others decided to go to Melon's bakery in Farnworth. Every morning they would leave trays of cream cakes and bread outside for the wagons to load up. We used to raid it and sell the cakes at school. We made a small fortune which we used to spend in the pub. It soon came to an end as they were waiting for us. I hadn't realised that some of us got caught.

I was inside one of their wagons helping myself to bread and cakes. When the wagon doors shut suddenly on me. The wagon set of with me inside and after about twenty minutes it stopped. The doors opened and I saw an unhappy driver. He grabbed me by my hair and dragged me out of his wagon. He was angry and he told me if I ever come back to Melons again he would inform the police and then he told me to fuck off. I didn't know where I was. The bastard dropped me off in the middle of Darwin, which was miles away from Bolton. It taught me a lesson. I never went back there again.

I started to get more and more into mischief at school. The more beatings I got at home from my dad, the more rebellious I would be come. I was uninterested in doing school work. I just wanted to have fun.

Bonfire day was just the excuse I needed. A couple of others and I (I won't mention their names for obvious reasons) took the day off school and we raided the paper shop to nick as many bangers and rockets as we could. We nicked a few bottles of milk and used the bottles as fire work launches for our rockets. We then headed for Harper Green school and we hid on the field so nobody could see us. When the school kids came out on the playground, we set the rockets off and aimed them just over the heads and when we ran out of rockets we threw bangers at them. The noises made them scatter in all directions. We rolled about laughing on the grass and when the teachers came out we just scarpered.

I failed my exams miserably I even tried to cheat a little by going to the toilet and writing the answers on my arms. I wasn't the only one practising this as the toilet was full of people doing the same.

Before I left school, I did get my little revenge on Mr Eckersley on my last day by letting down all his tyres on his car. I put a little letter on his windscreen with the words, *from your number one hated pupil* and signed with a few kisses.

I left school forever in April 1974. I walked through the school gates for the final time with some good memories, a few bad ones and an uncertain future. I went to the Grapes pub with a few friends, got drunk and made my way home.

I started work a few days later at William Walkers in Bolton. I was a young, boyish- looking sixteen-year-old; very immature with a rebellious nature. It would be the start of a new beginning for me it would be my first independence and money. It was the start of what would be a new chapter in my life

Chapter Twenty-Four

Brixham Bound

After years of physical and mental torture from my dad, my mum finally plucked up the courage to leave him. I remember the day well, it was a Saturday morning. Mark, Stephen, Pat and I were all in bed when my mum opened the door and woke us up. Mum whispered in my ear to get up quickly as we were all leaving and going to our Denise, my older sister in Brixham (South Devon.) She said she had had enough and was leaving my dad for good. I was so happy, I dressed as quickly as I could. I woke up Mark and Stephen and my mum woke our Pat up. My mum gathered a few belongings and packed them all in to one suitcase.

We all sneaked down stairs and in jest I said to my mum, "Where is my dad?"

She replied, "Don't worry about him, he's fast asleep." Apparently, she had put some sleeping tablets in his drink to knock him out which she did many times for a bit of peace and quiet.

We all sneaked out of the back door and it was there that I saw Father Melvin. I didn't realise at the at the time but my mum had confided in him about the troubles with my dad. Father Melvin was the local priest at Our Lady of Lourdes parish church on Plodder Lane. He was a lovely, kind and caring priest who once gave me a ticking off for not going to the church Mass so much.

He took us to Bolton Moor Lane Bus Station in his car and it was there we said our goodbyes. He cuddled and kissed every single one of us in turn and he then wished us all good luck and waved and then he left. Father Melvin sadly died a few years later. *R.I.P Father Melvin.*

My mum had little money and when the coach pulled on to the platform the driver got out and asked my mum for the tickets. My mum started sobbing and the driver took her to one side and it was then my mum poured her heart out to him about the abuse we were all receiving from my dad. The driver took pity on her and let us all on the coach for free. When the coach stopped off at the services the driver bought us all a drink and something to eat.

The trip would take over eight hours. It was a long drive down but it was a happy one knowing we were going to have a new life in Brixham and away from my dad's clutches for good. My mum was very tired but she smiled at us all the way to Brixham. I held her hand most of the way. I was so happy for my mum that she had finally built up the courage to leave my dad. I was so proud of her.

We arrived in Torquay where our Denise's husband John was waiting for us. He took us in the car to their house. My mum gave the coach-driver a cuddle and thanked him for everything he did for us all. We waved him goodbye as the coach left the station.

Brixham was one off the busiest fishing ports in the UK and a working town, but it's also a place where you can discover a range of arts and culture, excellent local food and some unique attractions. Brixham attracts visitors for its character, charm and combination of tradition and an enthusiasm for contemporary styles. Originally a Saxon settlement, Brixham was the landing place of William of Orange during the Glorious Revolution, and many of the town's inhabitants, who are descendants of the Dutch army, have Dutch surnames. Many of the street names in Brixham reflect the town's history, with some also bearing Dutch influences.

We arrived at our Denise's flat which was on top of a shop on Fore Street, the main road where all the shops and pubs were. It was also very near to the harbour and where the Golden Hind was anchored which was a replica of Sir Francis Drake's ship. He was of course. the famous Elizabethan admiral who helped to defeat the Spanish Armada in 1588.

Denise's flat was just two bedrooms but it was very excellently furnished. I called it posh. The only thing that used to annoy me were the bloody seagulls which flew constantly over our heads and released their droppings on our heads and the noises they made throughout the night.

It was late in the evening when we arrived so after we had had something to eat it, fish and chips, which John bought for us from a chip shop called Rios. While in Brixham we all frequented it from time to time.

In the morning, Stephen, Mark and I and went for a walk round Brixham. We even went on the Golden Hind for a while.

In the harbour, there was an arcade with slot machines. Now and again I used to bang the machines and on the odd occasion a few coins used to drop out. We did this on most of the machines for a while until I got caught and was banned from visiting the arcade.

We went fishing on the odd occasions on the breakwater next to the sea. I never caught any fish but it was fun nevertheless.

We walked up to the old Napoleonic fort on Berry Head. Berry Head, located west of Brixham in Devon, has been fortified since the Iron Age. It is a strategic high point covering the harbour of Brixham and the rest of Torbay. This was realised during the Napoleonic Wars, and three forts were constructed. They consisted of ramparts with long rows of guns, protected by dry ditches, and sheer cliffs (although one fort no longer exists.) We used to go there a lot and sit on the ruins and the old cannons and look across the sea. They reckon you could see France on a clear summer's day. I was so happy I never thought about school or especially my dad. I certainly didn't miss the hidings I used to get from him.

Brixham was paradise. John used to work in a restaurant called the Strand every day and if we went in, we got a cream cake. The only trouble I had was when I was playing football with my brothers when a young kid popped our ball. He got a slap on the head from me only to see him run off and bring his dad who was huge. He pinned me against a shop window and told me if I hit him again I would receive a special knuckle duster from him (slap.)

After about two weeks we was all sitting around the table having our dinner. A Cornish pasty, it was all meat with a few carrots. It was delicious. Then I heard someone coming up the steel steps. We all looked out and we could see a shadow and then a knock came on the door. Denise opened the door and to our shock it was my dad with a bunch of flowers. Denise wouldn't let him in at first but my mum interrupted and said she would speak with him. They both went in to the bedroom where they chatted for a while.

Then, we were all hit with a bombshell. My mum said, "We are all going home."

I started to cry and said, "Why mum? I like it here."

She replied, "We can't stay here. There is no room. We must go back. Your school is there and your dad has promised to look after us.

We took the train home. It was long and I was very quiet. I knew my mum and I were going back into a trap and no matter what my dad promised us, I didn't believe him as he was a bad liar. A leopard never changes his spots, I thought to myself.

After the train stopped at Birmingham a young man with black shoulder-length hair sat facing us. I got talking to him. It was no other than the young Trevor Francis who played for Birmingham City and would eventually play for England. We all got his autographs and we chatted all the way till he got off at Manchester.

Reality sunk in when we finally arrived at Bolton station. We caught a taxi to Derwent Road where we lived and as the taxi pulled up I looked at our house. I felt so numb I can't explain the feelings in my stomach, but what I can say is that when I walked through the door I felt a cold chill down my spine, as though I had seen a ghost. The house wasn't haunted but a bogeyman certainly frequented the place and he was the man I called my father.

It was peaceful for a few weeks but it didn't last long. My dad soon went back to his evil ways and the beatings would carry on for a little while longer.

Chapter Twenty-Five

The Infamous Sergeant Swann

Sergeant Swann was as tough as they come. He was six-foot tall and about twenty stone to match. He lived just at the top of my road in one of the police houses. Over the years, he would become a thorn in my side.

I crossed his path many times. It started from a young age and many times I would receive a clout behind the ear and be dragged to my mother's house where I would receive another good hiding from my dad for getting caught.

The first time our paths crossed was outside the shops. I was only nine years old. The shops were at the top of the road where I lived at the time. There was a newspaper shop a chip-shop and a post office and there was also a small Co-op mini-mart which was rich pickings for me and my school friends. We would fill our pockets with sweets on our way to school and as we got older and more daring would put bottles of cider under our jackets.

Anyway, I was with a number of my friends, playing football when I kicked the ball and knocked the Sergeant's helmet off. He went red in face and I could see he was getting increasingly angry that we were all laughing at him. It was like a red rag to a bull and he came storming over and clipped me round my ear and said, "You are not laughing now, are you?" He took our ball from us and just walked away laughing.

The second occasion when our paths crossed was when I and number of friends were caught pinching toffees from the penny tray. The owner of the shop reported us to police and we were held in the store room like criminals. I was 'shitting' myself and when the door opened and I saw Sergeant Swann he commented, "Well, well, well, who do we have here? It's our local Fagin and his little gang."

He took all our names and he wasn't happy to see me but he just smirked and told us to leave the shop. He told me specially that he would be making a visit to my house.

I started to worry what would my father do if he found out but for some reason the knock on my door never came.

I was getting into trouble now on what seemed to be a weekly basis for what seemed like trivial things; playing football, knocking on a door and running away and for just being a nuisance with the public.

It was always Sergeant Swann on the warpath. Once I was caught stealing coal from one of my neighbour's coal bunkers with my dad's blessing and received a good hiding from my dad for getting caught by the infamous Police Sergeant.

When I was thirteen years old, my four friends and I; I won't name as I don't want to embarrass them, stole three bottles cider from the paper shop.

We were all drinking it on the steps at the back of the Flying Shuttle which was our local pub. At the time the Flying Shuttle was infamous for its pub brawls. It was wrecked on many occasions and was only patronised by the local idiots.

Anyway, we were all getting drunk on the cider and having a laugh, making a nuisance of ourselves. It wasn't long before we came to the attention of Sergeant Swann. I don't know how he found us but somebody must have tipped him off. He came over to us with his usual sarcastic grin. I must admit I was 'shitting' myself, my legs were like jelly. He took the bottles from us and put them in a plastic bag to throw them in the bin. He took all our names, as usual, but this time he held me and told the rest of my friends to go home and said he would be making a visit to their parents. As they walked away he snarled at me and grabbed me by the ear and dragged me to my house which was only a few minutes away. Along the way, he kept telling me I was a pain in the backside and he was sick of me and that I was a problem to society.

I was at the door of my house and my stomach was doing summersaults. My legs were like jelly at the prospect of facing my dad.

Sergeant Swann knocked on door and to my shock my dad opened the door. Before I could speak Sergeant Swann told my dad that I had been drinking cider and making a nuisance of myself (true) and making obscene gestures at the public (a lie.)

He tried to give the impression to my dad that we had stolen the cider from the local co-op but he couldn't prove it

My dad told him he will sort me out and that I wouldn't be playing out for a very long time. This brought a huge smile to the Sergeant's face.

My dad dragged me through the door and punched me a few times and told me to go to my room and stay there.

I was glad I wasn't going to school as it was holiday time and I was sick of going with bruises on my face.

For the next few days I never went out and I only came down stairs to eat my meals.

My mum told me to start behaving myself and that I wasn't helping myself with my dad.

One day my mother received some bad news which rocked the whole family. My dad's mum who we called little nanny, had died. We all loved her very much. She had lived with us for a long time and mum used to look after her as she had had both legs amputated.

My dad was heartbroken on the day of the funeral. For whatever reason, he took his upset out on me and punched me in the face and blacked my eye.

I was shaking with fear and I was crying my eyes out. Only the intervention of my mother saved me from more punishment.

After the funeral I was determined to run away to France and my decision was made.

Back to sergeant Swann I wanted to get my own back on him so I had a plan of action. I bought a black spray from the local garage and I was going to put graffiti on the front of his house and get my ultimate revenge.

So, one night I sneaked out of the box-room window, which I had used for my escape, many times in the past.

I made my way up the road to Sergeant Swann's house. It was three o'clock in the morning. I sneaked up his path; made sure everybody was in bed and that there were no lights on in the house. Then I sprayed in big black letters 'Mini BWFC' which I would use as my status many times in local football grounds over the years.

I also sprayed, 'Sergeant Swann is a fat bastard,' in huge letters across the front of his house.

The job was now done and it was time to disappear. I made my way back to my house with a huge smile on my face I climbed up the drain pipe and through the window and sneaked into my bed with huge satisfaction on my face. Revenge was sweet, I said to myself.

A few days later I was walking up Derwent road with my mum when Sergeant Swann spotted us. He came running over to us. He was gesturing as he approached us. He was going crazy shouting, "I know it was you who vandalised my house and if I could prove it I would arrest you and have you charged."

My mum went berserk with him and accused him of harassing me and that she would report him. He marched off waving his arms and muttering under his breath. I had a huge smile on my face and I was so happy to get my ultimate revenge.

I kept a low profile after that and I tried to avoid him whenever possible.

Our paths did cross a few times over the next few years, however. The last time was on a field next to Anchor Lane in Highfield where I lived. It was a road which led to a flyover bridge into Little Hulton.

There were a good thirty lads from Highfield and we were having a bit of a stand-off with our hated enemies from Little Hulton the Spillymies.

There were over sixty lads from both sides having a free-for-all. Bottles and bricks were being thrown and some lads were carrying knives.

Then in the background we heard the police sirens and knew it was time to leave. The cavalry had arrived and they came armed with police batons and police dogs. It was time to run for our lives. I and another lad who I'll just call Liam ran through someone's garden.

Then we heard this loud voice shout my name and I turned around to see Sergeant Swann. He was threatening us both with arrest. He was knackered, red in the face and gasping for breath. Me and Liam just stopped and laughed at him and shouted, "You fat bastard, don't you think you need to retire now? You're passed it and so over-weight."

We just couldn't stop laughing as we trotted off. He was too exhausted to catch us.

That was the last time I crossed paths with Sergeant Swann. I did see him on various occasions later on and I couldn't resist muttering a few obscenities whenever I saw him.

He sadly died after I had moved away from Highfield. I never held any malice towards him. After all he was only doing his job and he was probably a decent bloke underneath that uniform.

R.I.P. Sergeant Swann. Thanks for all the fun we used to have together. I still chuckle to this day when I think about it.

Chapter Twenty-Six

The day I tried to end it all

The dark clouds seemed to be hanging over my house. Once again, I was in a deep depression. I was 14 years old and my drinking was getting out of control. I was becoming more rebellious by the day as I thought the whole world was against me. The abuse was constantly aggressive and violent. I tried to fight back against my father but I always came off second best. My mother was preoccupied, defending herself against my father. For a few months, I seemed to be happy. I met a girl called Mandy who was fifteen years old; very pretty, kind and caring, a sweet girl who was fun to be with.

Whenever we were together the depression and the heartache seemed to go away. Unfortunately, she was involved in a car accident and would eventually end up in a wheelchair and move to Bristol for a better life. I was heartbroken. I went back on the drink and as usual getting into mischief. Things didn't get any better between my father and me and I started to stand up for myself in a small way by being cheeky to him. This made him worse and the violence would start to get more extreme.

Things came to head one morning. I was late getting up. I was still missing Mandy and I was still upset. I was brushing my teeth in the bathroom when my father came storming in and just grabbed me and pushed me against the wall for no reason. He was banging my head against the wall without saying a word. I totally lost it. I yelled at him and said that he was monster. He looked at me with pure evil in his eyes. His face was distorted with rage. He went crazy and started punching me in the stomach. I dropped onto the floor in pain. I couldn't breathe. I screamed at him to stop but he carried on kicking me around my body for what seemed like ages but it was probably no more than just a few minutes. He then walked out of the bathroom laughing. I then heard the front door shut with a loud bang as though the door had come off its hinges. I was in total agony I crawled on my hands and knees into my bedroom and just lay on the bed.

My school jumper had been torn and my shirt collar was covered in blood. My legs were killing me. As for my stomach, I was struggling to breathe. My rib cage was swollen on one side and I could see bruises in that area. Every time I tried to breath I would get pain on my side. I slowly walked in into the bathroom. I could hardly walk after the hiding he gave me. I looked in to the mirror and my right cheek was badly swollen. I started to weep. I couldn't take it any longer. I just wanted the beatings to come to an end. All I wanted was a normal childhood and to be loved. I opened the bathroom cabinet and I picked up my dad's razor. I then I slumped down on to the toilet seat. Tears rolling down the side of my face, I pushed my jumper sleeve up and I started to slash my wrist and arms. I wanted to die. I just didn't want to live any more.

I don't know how long I was slashing my arms with the razor. I was totally oblivious to what I was doing or what was happing around me. I felt like I was in a trance.

I didn't realise my mother was there. She grabbed the razor out of my hand and screamed at me to ask what had happened? I just looked at her in the eyes and I didn't answer. She slapped my face to try to get a reaction. I felt weird as though I was drunk. The room was spinning around. I must have fainted because when I woke up my mum was wrapping my arms in a towel. I looked on the floor and it was covered in blood.

My mum just came straight out with it and said, "I'm taking you to hospital as you need stitches. Your arms are in a mess."

My mum lifted me up and I could feel the blood pouring down my arms. She took my jumper off and I yelled out in pain. She then put a shirt on for me. I couldn't move as my ribs were killing me.

I had to go down the stairs step by step aided by my mum because I was in agony and my legs were like jelly. She rang for an ambulance and it was here with a matter of minutes. My mum spoke to the ambulance driver outside the front door. I couldn't hear what they were saying but when the ambulance driver came in he pulled the towels off my arms. It was then that I saw the damage I was shaking and crying. I just couldn't remember slashing my arms. I must have been in a state of shock.

He then bandaged my arms. He asked me, "How did you slip on the broken windows panels? You have cut your arms really badly."

I just looked at him puzzled. My mum interrupted and said he was rushing out the door as he was late for school and he slipped and fell on to the window panels which were lying next to the coal bunker and it was all the broken glass that cut his arms and he hurt his ribs and banged his head as well.

I looked at my mum and agreed that is what happened exactly. I knew he didn't believe me as they were straight cuts and it was obvious there was no glass in my arms.

I was taken to Townleys hospital on Minerva Road which wasn't far from my house. In the ambulance, my mum held me in her arms all the way there. I was taken straight into a cubicle and it wasn't long before I was treated by a doctor and a nurse. They checked my arms and straight away I was told they were badly cut and they needed stitches. The doctor checked the side of my face and said it was badly swollen.

I told the doctor I was in pain at the side of my ribs and I was told I might have cracked or badly bruised ribs. My arms and wrist were stitched and I counted 63 stitches in all.

I also had an X-ray and I found out I had a cracked rib. I was in total agony I couldn't breathe properly.

The doctor and the nurse who helped to stitch me up knew something was untoward but I never told them what happened. I was too scared to say anything in case my dad took it out on my mum. For the next few months my mum would never leave my side. I understood why she lied to the ambulance driver and the hospital as it would have brought shame to my family. I never told anybody what happened; not even my closest family members or my best friends. It would be a secret that would be kept between me and my mum for all these years until now that I am writing my book. My mum would take the secret to her grave.

A few months later, after the incident, I decided enough was enough. I would run away to Paris with the intentions of never returning home. It would be the first time away from my mother and I would sail across the English Channel all alone and into an uncertain future.

Chapter Twenty-Seven

Paris, Freedom & Alone

When I was fourteen I decided enough was enough. I was fed up with the constant bullying from my dad. I wanted to be free and out of his clutches.

I had already saved up a bit of money and took more out of my dad's wallet every time he came home drunk. I had a total of thirty pounds. That was a lot of money in those days. I had a small rucksack to put a few bits of clothing and some food and drink into.

I had always wanted to go to France and Paris was the destination I chose. Now I had to have a plan of action and find out how I would travel there. I already knew I could get a sixty-hour excursion document from the ferry company as long I signed it as though I was 16 and if they were satisfied that I would be back in England before the sixty hours expired. Little did they know I had no intention of returning to England?

I planned to leave on the Saturday, in the early hours; all I had to do now was to try to stay out of my dad's way and keep out trouble.

I had tried to act normally with my mother but every time she smiled at me I felt like breaking down.

I had never been separated from my mother before and I felt very sad that I was running away but I had to go. I loved my mother so much and I felt like I was abandoning her.

I couldn't take the beatings any longer and being locked away from my friends.

I kissed her good night and hugged her very tight. I told her that I loved her very much and off I went to bed. I had to stay awake as I knew I was leaving in the early hours. I cried so much through the night as I just couldn't stop thinking about my mother.

But my mind was already made up. In the early hours of the morning I packed my rucksack with a few clothes and essentials and sneaked out of the box-room window once again. I jumped onto the ledge and then climbed down the drain pipe.

I looked at my mum's bedroom and my tears started to run down the side of my face. I turned around and I ran up Derwent Road like a bat from hell.

It was 5.30 in the morning and I had to find my way into Bolton and get there as quickly as possible before my mother found me missing.

I walked it to Bolton which was only a forty-minute walk and I made my way to Moor Lane which was our main bus and coach station.

I had already booked a coach to London Victoria station but it wasn't leaving until seven o'clock so I just waited the half hour sitting on a bench and deep in thought.

The half hour passed very quickly and it wasn't long before the coach for London Victoria arrived.

There weren't many people waiting and they were mainly old. The coach door opened and it was here that my adventure began. I climbed into the coach and showed my ticket to the driver. He just looked at me and nodded his head.

I went straight to the back of the coach and sat next to the window as the coach started to pull out of the bus station.

I suddenly felt all alone and I didn't want to think what lay ahead for me but I didn't feel afraid. I just felt relieved that I was finally free; free from fear and the hand of my father.

It wasn't long before we were on the motorway and Bolton was now a distant memory. I was heading for Paris on an adventure and a journey into the unknown.

I fell asleep and I slept nearly all the way and that was six hours solid.

We arrived in London on time and now I had to find where the coach was to Dover.

I found that I didn't need to ask strangers where the ticket office was. People were continually asking me if I was lost and if I was alright. I was only small for my age with a baby-face. This was becoming a hindrance no matter where I went.

Victoria Coach Station is the largest coach station in London. It serves long-distance coach services and is also the departure point for many countrywide coach tours originating from London.

I made my way across the station to where the ticket office was. For the first time, I noticed people begging which I had never seen before and people sleeping rough. Little did I know this would be the world I would be living in? I quickly purchased the ticket for Dover.

The trip to Dover was uneventful. It felt just as long as the journey from Bolton but it only took a few hours.

I purchased my ticket with much difficulty at the ferry-office. Not having a passport, I needed a special permit for a short visit to France. I had to convince the guy at the ticket office that my mother lived in Paris, and I was sixteen years old. When he started to question my story, I burst into tears.

I was so scared of being caught at this point but to my relief he gave me the pass.

I didn't have to wait long before I was boarding the ferry to Calais. I changed what little money I had into French Francs.

I looked into my rucksack and 'the cupboard was almost bare.' I ate and drank what was left. I then made my way to the top deck. I could just make out the white cliffs of Dover disappearing into the distance behind me. It was then that I started to cry uncontrollably. My feelings were all confused. Even though I was free from my father's abuse I couldn't help feeling sad that I was abandoning my mother.

I don't know how long I was crying but the famous white cliffs of Dover were now beginning to fade completely from my view. The ship was sailing for Calais. A new adventure lay ahead. It could only be better than the life I had left behind.

The ship docked at Calais. I was now free but alone. I made my way to the train station where I purchased my ticket to Paris.

I was soon to realise how naive I was because most French people didn't speak any English. I realised this all the more when I arrived in Paris.

The journey from Calais to Paris was long and boring as it was night-time and you couldn't see much in the darkness.

I slept most of the journey away and I was awakened by a guard on the train who tried to explain that I was now in Paris.

I wiped my eyes and nodded my head in a gesture of understanding and made my way off the train and just followed the crowd out of the station.

By now it was dark but still quite warm even though it was in the early hours and the crowds from the train started to disappear.

I decided that it was time to find somewhere I could sleep; where it was safe from prying eyes.

I started to walk up the nearest street I could find. I remember noticing the houses were different from the ones

I grew up with. They were huge and colourful and I noticed the windows were different; some of them looked like doors and the streets were narrow.

I noticed a large wagon covered with a green canvas cover just parked up. I lifted the canvas and peered in. Inside there were some articles of furniture and a few bits of carpet and cushions. They looked soft and inviting and I was so tired I soon fell asleep.

I awoke with the hustle and bustle as Paris began to wake up. For a second, I did not know where I was until I heard people speaking French.

I peered out the wagon to see if it was clear to jump out. It was and I started walking. By this time, I was hungry and thirsty. I could smell freshly baked bread so I followed my nose to a small bakery. The shop window display was full of different kinds of shaped breads.

I went inside and I noticed a man who was huge in size and had a large beard. I tapped him on the arm and asked him for a ham buttie.

He spoke in French and gestured to me. Obviously, he didn't understand what I was saying.

So, I pointed to some bread and ham and cheese and a bottle of water. I then showed him the amount of money I had left in my hand.

He shrugged his shoulders and made me the biggest ham and cheese sandwich I had ever seen. I thought it would last me all week.

The guy took every cent I had but I think now I got the better end of the deal as I suspect he took pity on me.

I stepped out of the shop and waved goodbye. I sat down on a bench tucking in to my ham and cheese buttie, watching the world go by.

I noticed tables and chairs on the pavement and people arriving drinking coffee. I found it strange but fascinating.

I wanted to see the Eiffel Tower which was supposed to be miles bigger than our Blackpool tower. I just started to walk. I don't know how long I was walking for but it seemed to be forever.

I asked passers bye and I tried to say Eiffel Tower. Most just walked past and shrugged their shoulders.

Eventually an elderly English couple took pity on me. They asked me why I was on my own. I told them that I had lost my parents and that I had no money and I was supposed to be meeting them at the Eiffel Tower.

I put on the waterworks and it worked. They gave me ten Francs and they took me to a bus-stop so that I could get a bus to the Eiffel Tower.

It wasn't long before a small bus arrived and I just followed the few tourists onto the bus. I was only small, so I could sneak onto the bus undetected, and I made my way to the back.

The journey to the centre of Paris didn't take long. I was in awe of the beautiful buildings and the architecture and I could see the Eiffel Tower in the distance.

When the bus arrived at the destination I just followed the crowds. I was overwhelmed by the sheer size of all the structures.

There were hundreds of cafés with tables outside and all the tables were full of people eating and drinking coffee.

You could smell the local pastries and garlic. By now I was getting hungry and thirsty. I was in my second day in Paris and I had very little money; all I had left was a few francs.

I went to one of the little shops in the square and all I could afford was a bottle of water. The shop was full, so I had to decide, pretty quickly. If I wanted to survive I needed food.

I opened my small jacket and put a couple of small loafs and some pieces of cheese under my arm. Then I made my way to the counter and paid for the bottle of water with the small change I had.

My heart was pounding and I was fearful of getting caught but to my surprise the shop owner just smiled at me.

I made my way out of his small shop with a massive grin on my face. I decided that I had to eat now as I was starving and thirsty as the heat of the day was scorchingly hot.

I sat down on and while I was eating I was looking at the thousands of tourists just walking about. They all spoke different languages as they came from all over the world.

I could see the Eiffel Tower in the distance. This was my next plan of action; I had to see one of the main attractions of Europe. I followed the crowds and headed for the Eiffel Tower. The walk would take me past museums and fancy shops and there were plenty of restaurants.

When I arrived at the huge Eiffel Tower there were literally thousands of people in large queues. I sat on the grass bank. I was just amazed at the beauty and splendour of Paris and its surroundings. I just laughed to myself as I thought how different it was to where I lived in Highfield.

It was getting on now; nearly nine pm in the evening and I was getting thirsty and hungry again.

I also had to find somewhere to sleep, so I was on the lookout for wagons that were parked up.

I headed for the narrow streets and away from the hustle and bustle of the crowds. I could smell the hot pastries and the smell of fresh bread was everywhere I went.

I passed what looked like apartment blocks and outside one of them was a large truck covered in blue canvass. I looked inside and it was empty so I decided to bed down there for the night.

I was tired and exhausted and I was still hungry and thirsty. I must have fallen asleep pretty quickly as I was awoken by the sound of traffic and the noise of passing people.

I peeped through the canvas and when it was all clear I jumped out and made my way up the narrow streets.

I passed a bakery and outside there were bread and pastries on trolleys. It was my chance to feed myself. I took what I could and disappeared before I got caught.

I headed for the embankment along the river Seine. I walked for miles and every now and again I would stop and watch the floating restaurants and tourist boats.

There were plenty of cafés and restaurants along the embankment. There were also hundreds of artists painting the scenic views.

I sat and watched them painting for a while. The heat of the day was scorching and I was very thirsty.

I was getting desperate. I needed water and food pretty quickly. I sat next to the embankment and I started begging.

People looked at me and just passed me by. I had to take desperate measures. I picked myself up and did something that was alien to me.

I tried to be a pickpocket and to steal out of people's handbags while they were busy looking at the shops and admiring the sights of Paris.

I wasn't getting anywhere. I was feeling sick with the hunger and thirst. It was now my third day in Paris and I was feeling alone, desperate and very weak.

I tried again to pick pockets but I was useless. Out of the corner of my eye I saw three black youths coming towards me. Before I could I decide, they were onto me like a pack of wolves. They slapped me across my face and grabbed me by the throat. I was shaking with fear. They were shouting at me in French and they threw my bag over the embankment and ran off.

I quickly realised that I must have been on their patch. I hastily walked away along the embankment with tears rolling down my face. My thoughts were now about my mother and my family but I was scared to go home and face the wrath of my father.

I was alone and frightened. I didn't know where to turn next; I was hungry and thirsty and very weak. I thought I was going to die. I was just desperate for food and water so I just walked straight into a shop and grabbed a bottle of water. It was then that I heard a loud voice in French. I turned around and it was all over. The shopkeeper grabbed me and took me into the backroom. He sat me down and I just looked at him. I was too weak to say anything.

He left the room and I put my head in my hands and I wept. I was interrupted by a hand on my shoulder. I looked up with my tired eyes to see two French police officers.

They told me in broken English to follow them as I was being taken to the police station.

As I passed the shop keeper he just smiled at me. He must have taken pity on me.

I arrived at the police-station in a police car. I put my head on the window and I just wept. I was tired and weak.

In the police station one of the officers rubbed my hair and then held my hand and took me further into the building.

I found myself in a small room with just a table and chairs. They left the room and after a short while an English-speaking officer came in.

He asked me how old I was. I told him I was fourteen. He then asked me why I was here in Paris and how did I get here.

I told him I had run away from home because I wasn't getting on with my father. He then replied that I was lucky not to be charged as I was under age.

While I was talking to him another police officer came in with a bottle of coke and a ham sandwich. I was then told that after I had eaten and cleaned myself up I would be taken to the British Embassy and they would make the necessary arrangements to get me home.

It was a short journey across Paris and I was now sight-seeing in comfort but I knew my adventure was coming to an end.

I had a smile on my face I had probably done what most children wouldn't do in a lifetime and I felt proud of that.

I had done things alien to me in desperation to survive but I was glad now it was coming to end. I was happy that I was going back home to be near my family and at that time I didn't care about facing the wrath of my father.

I arrived at the Embassy and I was met by an Embassy official. He took me inside the building and showed me a room with a bed in it. He then told me I would be sleeping there for the night and that I would be going home to England in the morning.

I was taken into a room and he asked me lots of questions; why I came to Paris and how did I get there? I just smiled and replied I always fancied coming to Paris and that I had a bet at school with my friends.

I lied to him as I knew I would be going home to my family and I didn't want them asking any questions about my father.

He just smiled and said it was time to ring my parents and he asked me what the number was? He gave me a piece of paper and I wrote the number down.

The embassy official then telephoned my mother and spoke to her. "We have your son," he informed her.

"Why? Where is he?" my bewildered mother asked.

"He's in Paris."

There was silence before I heard my mother exclaim, "Paris? I'll bloody kill him when he gets home!"

Looking back, it seems I was never afraid of striking out on my own to find pastures new.

I don't remember much about the trip home. I know I travelled by coach and ferry. When I finally got home my mother was waiting for me.

I knocked on the door and my mother opened it. She burst out crying and held me in her arms. She told me that the police had been looking for me and that they had searched the house and even the attic.

She held me and made me promise that I wouldn't run away again. I cried in her arms and said I was sorry.

That was the end of one journey and little did I know that a few years later I would be going on another one that would turn out to be a bigger nightmare and one I certainly wouldn't forget.

Chapter Twenty-Eight

Camping Out on Piggy

I always wanted to go camping I could never afford a tent and a sleeping bag but I always liked the idea sleeping out and having a laugh with my friends. There were plenty of fields near my house where we could pitch a tent and be out of sight and out of mind.

At the beginning, the closest I would ever get to camping on a field would be my back garden at the grand old age fourteen years old and my dad would still keep an eye on me through the window.

When the night arrived, Frank and I set up the tent in the middle of our garden. I brought down some blankets and a pillow from my room. Frank had a sleeping bag. It was quite a pleasant night so it wasn't cold; June can be quite warm. In those days, summers were summers and winters were winters. Frank had smuggled some cider bottles in his sleeping bag to help us through the long night. We lit a couple of candles in the tent so it was light and we could see each other. I also had a torch if the candles burned out.

Frank pulled a cider bottle out and we took it in turn drinking it.

Frank said to me have a guess what he had brought; an Ouija board. I must admit, I wasn't comfortable about the idea. You hear the stories about how dangerous Ouija boards are, but hey — it's just a game. Frank waited until midnight to begin our little game, and the two of us started by asking all kinds of silly questions. It was a strange-looking board, covered with letters and symbols. There was a plastic pointer that was supposed to move across the board at the behest of the spirits. The instructions called it a planchette. Around one thirty in the morning, the planchette suddenly froze in Franks hand. It wouldn't move, no matter how much we pushed and pulled. I was terrified. That was the end of that. I threw it out of the tent and it was the last time I would set eyes on it. Frank thought it was hysterical. I didn't.

We finished off the two bottles of cider and had a little laugh shining the torch on and off through our neighbours' windows.

The next time I went camping was when I was fifteen years old. Frank and I had planned to spend the night camping on Piggy but this time with two guests, Leslie and Carol who we knew from the estates near me. I told my mum and dad I was staying at my auntie Ann's and she covered for me with my mum. Frank's mum was ok and wasn't as strict. As for our two guests, they told their mums they were staying at each other's houses. Frank made sure it was in the hottest month of August so it stayed light till late and it was dry.

I arranged to meet Frank at 6.30 near Cherry Tree School on Highfield Road. It was out sight of my mum and it wasn't far from Piggy. I made sure I had a bottle of cider, I nicked it from Jacks, and a couple of blankets, I smuggled out of the house. When I arrived, Frank was already there with Leslie and Carol. Frank was all over Carol, he couldn't keep his hands off her until I told him to stop it and save it for later. Leslie was the opposite of Carol. She was quite shy, a bit tubby with long blonde hair but with huge breasts which I liked. She wasn't much to look at but, hey, you know the saying, "You don't look at the mantelpiece when you poke the fire."

Carol was stunning she had long brown hair and was as fit as a butcher's dog. Not much up top but I could have handled that. We all set off and headed for Piggy. We made sure we pitched the tent in the middle of the field. The tent was quite big as it was a four- man tent and it took us a good thirty minutes setting everything up.

Leslie had a white t-shirt which you could see straight through which didn't take long to get me going. Carol was wearing a thick white blouse with white shorts, she looked amazing. Frank knew I fancied her but he also knew I wouldn't do anything behind his back. Frank brought a bottle of vodka. The girls brought with them one bottle of cider and a bottle of lemonade to go with the cider. Frank also brought a gas lamp for when it was dark, a radio with batteries of course, so we could have laugh, dancing to the music with the girls. He also brought some sausages and eggs with a loaf and a small frying pan. All we needed was to make a small camp fire to cook them.

Frank told Carol he had forgotten to bring his sleeping bag.

This brought a smile from Carol and who replied, "You can sleep in mine Frank, I don't mind."

I looked at Leslie and smiled and she just put her head down. The tent was all set up now after a few failed attempts at erecting it. We collected some wood to make a camp fire and Frank started to cook the sausages and then the eggs. The smell of burning sausages made me hungry. The girls had their eggs and sausages first, then we had ours. They tasted delicious, especially when you washed them down with cider and lemonade with a mixture of vodka. We all sat round the campfire having a laugh listening to the radio now and again. We would get up and dance round the fire. It was fun and we had a really good laugh. Time was getting on now it was nearly one in the morning.

After a while the drink started to get to me. I felt dizzy so I said to Frank lets go in the tent and play spin the bottle. "You know the score; whoever it lands on has to take something off."

This didn't go down too well with Leslie."

Carol was well up for it. Frank spun the bottle and it landed on Carol. To my amazement, she took her white blouse off first and my eyes started to pop out when I could see her white ample breasts in her skimpy white bra.

I was well up for this now. I started to spin the bottle faster and if it landed on me I couldn't wait to get my clothes off, as I wasn't shy and up for almost anything.

The cider bottles were now empty and all that was left was a small bottle of vodka which we took turns in drinking. The girls were getting quite tipsy and Leslie wasn't as shy as she was with all the alcohol she had drunk. I was down to my underpants. Frank was the same. Carol was down to her little pink knickers. As for Leslie, she was still in her white t-shirt and white knickers. By this time, I was feeling quite randy and it wasn't just the drink. I cheated a little and made sure the bottle landed on Leslie. It was time to take her top off to which she did within a split second. I couldn't keep my eyes off her huge breasts which were bulging out of her white bra.

Frank took matters in his own hands and decided to kiss Carol passionately and they climbed into her sleeping bag.

I was getting very aroused. I wanted a bit of the action. I started to kiss Leslie passionately with my tongue which soon aroused her. I could hear Carol moaning with pleasure so I just grabbed Leslie and we climbed inside the sleeping bag. She whispered in my ear and said she was a virgin. I just smiled and said, "Don't worry, I will be gentle with you and carried on kissing. "I unclipped her bra and started to fondle her breasts at the time. I could feel her hand on my crotch. It was now time for deep penetration. I couldn't wait any longer. I climbed on top of her and that was it. I set off like an electric train. This carried on for a good five minutes and I was bloody knackered. Leslie couldn't get enough of it.

I was oblivious to what Frank and Carol were doing. Leslie and I were half-pissed and we were both knackered. I felt her breasts for a while and we had a few French kisses to finish it off and then we fell asleep.

I was woken up early in the morning as I could smell burning I jumped up and the tent was on fire. Frank had forgot to turn the gas lamp off and he had kicked it over in his sleep. I jumped up and woke up Frank and the girls and we all dashed out with our clothes. Within minutes the tent was burnt to a cinder. We were lucky to get out without any serious burns. We quickly got dressed it was light now. It was 7. 30 in the morning and we soon calmed down and laughed it off. Not so much Frank, as he had to do some explaining. It was his dad's tent. We sat on the grass for a while and chatted for a bit. I wanted seconds with Leslie but she had sobered up now and she wasn't very obliging. The only thing I got was a little kiss and a small grope to my disapproval. We all decided it was time to leave. We said our goodbyes and I carried on to my auntie Ann's and slept for most of the day. It was the first and the last time I would ever go camping on Piggy. I enjoyed the adventure and the little romps with Leslie. It would carry on for little while longer with the odd knee trembler. As for Carol, she packed Frank in and got her mittens into a lad from across the bridge, our arch enemies the Little Hultoners, much to Frank's displeasure.

Chapter Twenty-Nine

Facing my Demons

As I progressed through my teens the abuse and the troubles I got into were taking over my life. I was just 15 years old and the beatings from my father were still relentless. I was looking for a way out, and the only way I could cope with all my demons was drinking alcohol which seemed to kill the emotional pain I was going through at the time.

Things came to a head and I remember the day very well. It was a Friday morning and my last day at school before the summer holidays. I got up late as usual for school, which didn't go down too well with my father. He had been drinking the night before and he was still the worse for wear.

He shouted up from the bottom of the stairs in his loud voice, "Ian, get up now, you are late for school." I just ignored him, thinking my mum would come up and get me out of bed, not knowing my mum was at the corner shop buying some milk for our breakfast. I could hear someone coming up the stairs. I thought it was my mum but I had a shock when I saw my dad. I could see he was angry by just looking at his face. It was distorted and I knew then I was going to get a good hiding again. He grabbed me by the hair and dragged me out of the bed and he just laid in to me. I was screaming at the top of my voice telling him I was sorry and not to hit me but he kept punching me all over my body. I could feel the blood pouring down my face from my nose. I was in complete agony and I just lay on the floor cringing and in a ball trying to cover and protect my face. He stopped after a few minutes which seemed like an eternity. Then he just walked away without saying a word to me. There was nobody in the house as my brothers and sister had already left for school.

I went in to the toilet and looked in the mirror and my face was covered in blood I just burst out crying I was shaking and I didn't realise I had soiled my pyjamas which stank. I was worried my dad would come back up and give me another beating. I sat down naked in the toilet and locked the door. I was too afraid to come out and face my dad. It would be nearly 15 minutes before I heard my mum's voice. She just came upstairs and tried to open the door. I let her in and she just looked at me in shock. She held me in her arms and started to cry which made me worse. I told her what happened and she just shouted down stairs at my dad that he was a monster and should be locked up.

This made me wet myself as I was scared he would take it out on her but my dad never responded, to my relief. My mum told me I wouldn't be going to school which was a relief as my face looked a mess and she didn't want the school asking any questions in case they informed the authorities. She hugged me and said one day you will stand up to your dad and give him a good hiding and he will never touch you or me again. That very prophecy would come true and it would be the biggest shock of his life. My mum quickly cleaned me up and told me to stay in my room for a bit and to keep out of my dad's way until he calmed down. I cried for over an hour I just wanted the abuse to stop it was a nightmare that I thought would never end. I couldn't tell anyone what was going on in case my dad found out and I was worried he would take it out on my mum so I kept quiet about it. Only my close circle of friends knew what was going on and I told them to keep it a secret.

After I calmed down I decided I was going for a drink. I knew I had no money and that I would have to sneak out of the box-room window to get out. I quickly got dressed and I deliberately put my long black thick coat on knowing too well I would have to steal a bottle of cider as I had no money. It would be easy to conceal it with the coat I would be wearing.

I crept out my room and looked over the banister to see if I could hear my mum and dad but it was all quiet so I sneaked into the box-room, opened the window and jumped onto the ledge and then jumped onto the path. I then ran like the bat from hell up Derwent Road.

I headed to Jack's shop on Plodder Lane where a few of my school friends and I used to help ourselves to a few things on my way to school. It wasn't difficult to steal anything as Jack was in his late sixties and was very trusting. He was actually, a nice bloke. He had whitish hair and was thin as a rake and was very small which made it easy to nick anything I wanted.

I arrived at Jack's shop which was on the corner of Plodder Lane and facing Our Lady of Lourdes School which was the infant and junior school I used to go to. I just walked straight in and I saw Jack. He was busy serving a few customers. This gave me ample opportunity to head straight for the alcohol. I had a quick look to make sure nobody was watching me and I took the first bottle which was whisky. I quickly put in under my coat and headed straight for the door. I had a quick look to see if Jack was looking but he was still busy serving the customers. I made my way to what we called the Dell. It was a playing field just of Highfield Road. I knew it well as I used to hide there when I used to skip school and church mass. It was also away from prying eyes as I knew not many people would be there.

It was quite warm so I lay on the grass and I just started drinking out of the bottle. It was the first time I had tasted whisky. It was disgusting but I carried on drinking it. I started to feel unwell. I felt dizzy and I started to vomit. I didn't realise that the whisky was a very strong drink.

I started to walk and make my way to Highfield Road. I climbed up the grass banking and started to walk down Highfield Road. I had the intention of going home and sneaking back in to sleep it off. I could feel myself going and the next thing I remember was being waken up in hospital with a couple of nurses putting a tube down my throat and pumping some stuff in the tube which made me vomit into a bucket. This went on for several minutes. It was a terrible experience which I would never forget. I felt so ill I couldn't walk, so they put me in a wheelchair and pushed me into a ward. Then they put me in a bed. It would be a matter of hours before I woke up and I remembered my mum holding my hand crying and saying to me why are you trying to kill yourself? I remember asking my mum where was I and what happened?

She replied, "You are in Bolton Royal hospital and you have just had your stomach pumped." A lady rang an ambulance because they found you on the side of the road unconscious. I just looked at her face and she was heartbroken. She thought I was going to die. She made me promise that I would stop drinking because it would kill me in the end. I had to admit I was frightened, and I knew I was heading towards a point of no return. I held my mum's hand. I cried so much. I told her I was fed up of being beaten by my father and the drink was the only thing that soothed my pain. She leaned over to me and held me in her arms and we cried together. She kept saying to me that she promised the abuse would come to an end and that if it happened again she would get my dad arrested and put away in prison where he belonged.

Of course, the abuse didn't stop and it would carry on for a little longer. I stayed in for another night and in the morning my mum picked me up from the hospital and took me home. My dad was fine with me for a short while but it didn't last long. As for the whisky I never touched it again; even the smell of it makes me feel sick.

The experience would always stay with me and of course I still got drunk but that wasn't difficult as I couldn't drink like most people. That's where the saying light-weight comes from.

Chapter Thirty

The Great Nat Lofthouse

From the tender age of just four, my mum and grandad used to tell me tales about Nat Lofthouse.

My mum used to talk about Nat Lofthouse with such pride and with a twinkle in her eye and tell me that he was a close family friend. I used to listen with such great anticipation that Bolton wanderers became the club that was close to my heart.

I started putting pictures of Nat Lofthouse in a scrapbook, together with everything connected with Bolton Wanderers. I even filled my side of the wall in the bedroom with posters of Nat Lofthouse and the club. This caused friction with my brother Mark who was an Everton fan and still has a soft spot for them, to this day. He had all the pictures of the Everton players of that era and we used to end up fighting on occasions because he used to taunt me with Everton football songs and rip my posters off my wall which is why I hate Everton so much.

Anyway, back to Nat. He was born in Bolton, Lancashire, in 1925. He joined the town's main club on 4th September 1939 and made his debut in a wartime 5–1 win against Bury on 22 March 1941 when he scored two goals. It was then more than five years until he made his league debut for the club, but he eventually played against Chelsea on 31 August 1946, when he scored twice in a 4–3 defeat. Lofthouse would go on to play 33 games for England, but his debut on 22 November 1950 made him 25 years old when he finally broke into the team. He perhaps justified a claim to an earlier call-up by scoring both goals in a 2–2 draw against Yugoslavia at Highbury on his debut.

On 25 May 1952, Lofthouse earned the title 'Lion of Vienna' after scoring his second goal in England's 3–2 victory over Austria. In doing so he was elbowed in the face, tackled from behind, and finally brought down by the goalkeeper. Back from national team duty, he then scored six goals in a game for the Football League against the Irish League on 24 September 1952.

In 1952–53, he was named FWA Footballer of the Year. He scored a goal – but was on the losing side – in the famous 1953 FA Cup Final (aka 'The Matthews Final') having previously scored in each round. That season he topped the First Division goal-scoring charts with 30 goals. He featured in the 1954 World Cup side. Lofthouse scored twice against Belgium in a match that ended 4–4. Injured for the next match, in the quarter final game against Uruguay he equalized in the 16th minute, after receiving the ball in the 18 yard box.

On 3 May 1958, almost five years to the day after losing the 1953 final, he captained Bolton in the 1958 FA Cup Final against Manchester United. There was a national wave of sympathy for United, who three months earlier had suffered grievously in the Munich air disaster. Bolton won the game 2–0 with Lofthouse scoring both goals, the second of which was highly controversial and remains a talking point to this day. Lofthouse went into a challenge with the United keeper Harry Gregg and barged him into the net to score. Shoulder charging the goalkeeper was a legitimate tactic at the time, but Lofthouse later admitted that his challenge was a foul.

On 26 November 1958, Lofthouse made his final England appearance, against Wales, at the age of 33, and he officially retired from the game in January 1960 because of an ankle injury, although his final league game was not until 17

December of that year, when he suffered a knee injury against Birmingham City. Lofthouse stands seventh in the list of English football's top division goals scorers. My mum and grandad told me that Nat used to come around to her house on Baxendale street in Astley Bridge every Sunday for his dinner and talk about Bolton Wanderers and the goals he scored

My mum was so proud to have known Nat she used to get a lump in her throat and a bit tearful whenever she talked about him. I really used to look forward going to my grandparents not just because they used to treat me by buying me toffees, but because my grandad was a Bolton wanderers fanatic, I always listened with enthusiasm about the times he went to watch Bolton Wanderers and the great Nat Lofthouse at Burnden park. Nat was his idol and close friend. He always told me he disliked Manchester United and I think the rivalry has carried on through the generations of my family.

My grandad was a real character and in his broad Bolton accent he used to say, " Sit thee down lad," which brought a large smile to my mum's face. "I'll tell thee some stories about Nat. He went to the same school as your uncle Alf and I tell thee na', Alfred was a better footballer than Nat."

I looked at him with disbelief. I thought he was spinning me a yarn like he did about a German pistol my uncle Jim brought home from the Second World War. He told me he buried it in the back garden but I could never find it.

My grandad, however, was deadly serious. I later found out my uncle Alf was a very good footballer and so was his son who played professional football for Bury and various other clubs throughout his career.

My grandad told me Nat used to walk to Burnden park every day with his football boots tied round his neck and that he was proud of his Bolton background and that he loved the Bolton people. He also told me that Nat liked home-made ginger beer after his tea which was usually chicken and potatoes, along with my grandma's current buns which I tried once and they were like rock cakes, they were so hard. Nat must have had a hard set of teeth.

I had the pleasure of meeting the great Nat Lofthouse outside the players' entrance of Burnden Park years later. I spoke to him a few times and I mentioned my mum and grandad and my uncle Alf. He asked me their surname.

I replied, "Swales." He grinned and said what a lovely family the Swales were and Alfred was a good footballer. He winked and smiled at me when I mentioned my grandma's currant cakes.

Then he nodded his head and said. "Bye son, give my regards to Irene." Irene was my mum and then he went.

I told my mum what Nat had said and that made her day. She had the biggest smile in Farnworth, she felt so proud that day. Nat Lofthouse was her idol and I must admit, he was mine to and he was lovely bloke and really down-to-earth, a really nice guy who loved Bolton wanderers and was very proud of his Bolton heritage. Nat died on the 15th of January 2011. It was a sad day for everybody who had connections to Bolton Wanderers and specially for my mum who went to his funeral on that sad day in the team's history.

Chapter Thirty-One

Alone and in the dock

In 1973 I was arrested and charged by Bolton police for a disturbance on Manchester Road outside Bolton Wanderers football ground.

Before the game between Bolton Wanderers and Blackburn Rovers, I was taken to Bolton central police station. There I was interviewed with my mum present and charged with a breach of the peace. A form of Disorderly Conduct (threatening or using abusive or obscene language in a public place.) It wasn't a serious offence but never the less it was still serious enough for some form of punishment. I couldn't be tried in an adult court so I had to go to special court for youth offenders which today are known as juvenile courts. I was still classed as a minor. I had just turned 15 at the time and I was already out of control and very rebellious and I had a back ground of fighting at school and in various gangs since the age of nine. My father toughened me up without ever realising it, after all beatings I received from him from the age of four. I would eventually get my revenge and finally turn the tables on him in the months ahead.

On the morning of the game, which was on a Saturday and on a cold February day, I had my usual punch in the face for being cheeky with my father about something of nothing really. He just punched me in my face a couple of times which bruised the side of my left cheek which, "bloody-well hurt, I could tell thee." It swelled up quite a bit and after a while my eye started to blacken.

I just stormed out of the house and the usual abuse followed me. "If you don't come back you will get plenty more," which was my dad's favourite saying. I ignored his warning and took my chance and ran up Derwent Road. I sat down on a bench at a bus stop with my head in my arms sobbing.

An old lady in her late 70s came up to the bus stop and sat down next me. "You ok child, why are you crying?"

I just looked at her and replied. "I slipped on the road and I'll be fine don't worry." I smiled at her and I headed for my friend's house. Mick lived on Tig Fold. It was an old council estate and not far from me. I saw Mick playing football in the street with Frank, and I just casually walked over to them.

They both looked at me in utter horror and Frank just blurted out, "Your face looks a right mess. You been falling out with your dad again Mini?" This was my nickname.

I just smiled and said, "Listen, Bolton play Blackburn today. You both fancy going? We can have a laugh and watch all the aggro (fighting) before and after the game.

On the way, we called on Dave who was quite a character. He was a lot taller than us and had a lot more muscle than any of us. He was the kind of lad you would need if you got yourself into any scrapes (trouble).

We headed for Manchester Road and waited outside Bolton Train Station to see if we could see any Blackburn supporters hanging around. It was pretty quiet. There was just the odd Bolton fan walking around so we all headed in to the town centre for a bite to eat. I was skint but Mick as usual had money. We all had chips and pea juice which was quite common in those days.

Time was getting on now and it was around about 2.30 when we heard a loud commotion (noise) near the train station. That was enough for us to run towards the train station. There we saw a large group of lads fighting. There must have been two hundred of them in a free-for-all,

I didn't know who was who, but one lad came running past me with a few lads chasing after him. He was a Blackburn fan. I could tell by the blue and white scarf he was wearing around his arm. He was shitting himself. He looked a lot older than me. He was wearing a black jumper with white skinners (pants) with large black boots which seemed to go half way up his legs. Even though he was scared out of his wits he still looked quite menacing to me as he was a lot bigger than me. For whatever reason, I just hit out at him as he passed. The punch connected and he fell over onto the road. More and more lads were running towards my direction. It was quite obvious; the Blackburn lads had started to run for their lives followed by the Bolton fans in hot pursuit.

It wasn't long before the police sirens could be heard. This was the signal for everybody to depart and they just ran in all different directions. I lost Mick and Dave so I casually started to walk back into town. Then a police car pulled up and two police officers jumped out followed by the Blackburn supporter I had hit earlier.

He pointed at me and said to one of the police officers, "That's him who hit me earlier."

One of the police officers grabbed me and pushed me against the wall and told me that I was being arrested for being part of the fracas (fighting) outside the train station. I tried to plead my innocence but they wouldn't have it. They dragged me into the car and onto the back seat. They let the Blackburn fan go but not before he gestured and laughed at me as he walked away. They then took me to Bolton central police station. On arrival I was taken to the front desk and I had to give them my details and my mum's and dad's. I was taken into a small room and was told they would contact my parents and I would be interviewed later.

After an hour, I was taken into a special interview room. Inside I could see my mum and two police officers sitting at a table. They asked me a few questions about the fighting with the Blackburn supporters earlier and could I explain the marks on my face and assault on the Blackburn supporter? I told them that my father assaulted me and that I was with friends, walking past the police station when I was attacked.

I was shitting myself and my mother held my hand and had a go at one of the officers who was writing everything down and told them, "My son is telling the truth." The interview lasted over an hour during which time I was told I was being charged with breach of the peace and that I would have to attend a special court for youth offenders (juveniles) and then I would get the chance to plead my innocence.

My mother believed me and told me not to worry and that everything would be fine but I must keep out of my father's way for a while. I arrived home and my dad was waiting for me. As soon as he opened the door he hit me across my face and told me to get upstairs and stay there and that I was banned from going out for a whole month.

After three weeks, I received a letter with a date to attend court. For six weeks, I kept a low profile. I went to school and at home I stayed in my room.

The day had arrived I had to go to court and face the consequences. We caught the bus into Bolton and my mum tried her best to make me laugh which I was in no mood to do as I was shitting myself. We arrived at the building and we waited outside the special court room. I was quite smart. I had my hair cut and I was wearing a brand-new jumper and black pants my mother had bought me. I looked around and there was a young kid with his father. He looked as young as me. His father was shouting at him and calling him every name under the sun. It was soon interrupted when a man came out and shouted my name and I was told to follow him inside. In the room was a large brown table with three elderly men sitting behind it. There was also a woman sitting alongside a small table. She was writing things down.

Facing them, there were a few wooden benches. I was told to sit down. I looked around and there were a few pictures on the wall, all of them were of the Queen.

I began to get very nervous in fact I felt nauseous. One of the men told me to stand up and give my name.

I replied, "Ian Minihane, Sir." I was very nervous and he told me to speak up as they could not hear me. I was then asked the same sort of questions I had been asked in the police station. "Why was I at the train station?"

I replied, "I was with friends going into town, sir."

"How did you get the marks on your face?"

I replied, "The Blackburn supporter hit me sir."

I started to get upset and I just shouted out, "I'm telling the truth."

"Did you hit the Blackburn supporter?"

I said, "No Sir, I'm only small and he was a lot bigger than me. I was frightened and I tried to run away but he grabbed me."

I broke down and I started sobbing.

My mum stood up and held me, then sat me down. The questions carried on for about 15 minutes all the time the three elderly men in turn were firing questions at me.

They then told my mum to stand up they asked her name and asked her a few questions about my school and my general behaviour. All the time the woman was writing everything down.

We were told the hearing would be adjourned till 2.30 and we had to come back at that time and we would hear their final decision.

We went for a walk together around town, till it was time to go back. My mum was pretty confident of them being lenient with me and that I had nothing to worry about. I was innocent and even though I was mischievous, I was a good boy.

The few hours soon passed and it was now time to go and face the music. We arrived on time and we just sat down when the same man came out the room and said could you both follow me please and sit down. We both walked in and the men were already sitting down, waiting for us. Straight away one of the elderly men, the one who was sitting in the middle who seemed to be in charge, said, "We have come to a decision. There is insufficient evidence and this means you will be getting an absolute discharge and that you are free to go home." I broke down crying. I was expecting the worst.

My mum just smiled and said, "Thank you sir," and we both left the room.

I was so relieved and my mum was so happy she kept hugging me.

I just smiled at her and told her, "Thank you for being there for me." I told her that I loved her very much. I knew I was guilty and I was hurting her with all the trouble I was getting in to, but I couldn't stop myself. I was stubborn and very rebellious because of my father who was beating me up on a regular basis. At the time, I thought it was just a bit of fun. I didn't mean to hurt my mother who always stood by me and protected me.

It wouldn't be the last time I would cross paths with the police or the last time I would break the law it would carry on for a few more years.

Chapter Thirty-Two

Bolton Wanderers

Ever since I was young enough to remember, Bolton Wanderers was the club that was close to my heart.

The chats I had with my mum and my uncle Alf about Nat Lofthouse and Bolton Wanderers eventually led me on a roller-coaster ride of football violence and the road to self-destruction.

I was brought up in a house full of violence, looking at the clock and living in fear of my dad coming home drunk and giving me a good hiding. My dad was very strict and he had ground rules I had to obey and if I didn't follow them I was beaten and locked away in my room. I wasn't allowed to have fun like normal children and I wasn't allowed to bring girls home. Therefore it was natural for me to rebel against my father's wishes. I just wanted to be free and live a normal life, but the constant beatings and living in fear made me into someone I didn't want to be. My father made me violent and rebellious. I was getting involved in gangs and street fights. At the time, I thought it just looked normal. I didn't realise I was jumping out of the frying pan and into the fire. I was immature and a young kid who was rebelling against his father. I was getting rid of my frustrations on other people. This was one way of coping with it. I was already battle hardened with the scars to prove it. My father toughened me up after all the beatings I received, without ever knowing it and eventually I would turn the tables on him.

I had already had dealings with the police after my shenanigans with the infamous Sergeant Swann and my first football arrest when I was just 15 years old at the game between Bolton Wanderers and Blackburn Rovers at Burnden Park.

I saw mass disorder at Burnden Park in the early days. It would become a regular occurrence on most Saturdays.

Aston Villa

I first ventured to a game with friends when I was still at school. It was a game between Bolton Wanderers and Aston Villa. We couldn't go in to the game as we had no money. Aston Villa was a big club and I knew they would bring a large following of hooligans.

Before the game a few school friends and I were standing outside the Wagon and Horses. This was a pub on Manchester Road adjacent to the football ground.

I saw a large group of lads marching down Manchester Road surrounded by a few police with dogs. There must have been a good three hundred lads singing football songs. They were very loud and rowdy which attracted a few Bolton fans to come out of another pub, The Rose and Crown. The two sets of fans clashed and were fighting all over the road. The Villa fans chased the few Bolton fans back into the pub. The police had their work cut out but they soon had it all under control.

After the game, I was standing near the Embankment side when the gates were kicked open. Hundreds of Villa fans charged over to the Home end. They attacked the Bolton fans who were coming out of the ground and charged them back into the ground. After a loud roar, the Bolton fans ran out and attacked the Villa fans, it was one mass brawl. I watched with amazement as two sets of opposing fans ran into each other with such ferocity. Fist and kicks were there aplenty. I saw one fan go down on the floor after he was hit with a bottle and was knocked unconscious. It seemed to go on for ages before the police on horseback and a few with dogs chased them off.

The Villa fans were then marched back to the train station under police protection, but they still kicked off all the way to the train station.

Manchester City 1971

In 1971 I was still at school. I was just 13 years old. I was already battle hardened after being involved in gang fights with the Little Hultoners and various other factions. The next game I went to was Bolton Wanderers against Manchester City in the league cup tie at Burnden Park. There was a massive crowd on that night over 43,000 and a good contingent from Manchester. I didn't go into the game as I had no money, so a few friends from school and I climbed up the old scoreboard at the back of the embankment. The atmosphere was electric! We won the game 3-0.

After the game, we made our way to the Lever end on Manchester Road. We heard a loud roar inside the ground with echoes of Bolton Aggro. Bolton Aggro which echoed through the night air. The next thing hundreds of lads came piling out of the Lever end. The Bolton fans had chased them out of the home end. They showed no mercy to the City fans. They were attacked from all sides with bricks and bottles. It was a complete free-for-all. There were lads everywhere covered in blood with head wounds. I became caught up in the melee and I ran into a shop doorway. I saw a lad run straight past me. It was Mick from Highfield. He was chasing a City fan with an iron bar. God knows where he had found that. It seemed to go on for ages until the police got it all back under control.

Luton town 1973

Another game I went to was with my dad when Bolton Wanderers played Luton Town in the FA cup third round in front of nearly 40.000. It wasn't the game that excited me which incidentally we lost 1-0, it was the fighting in the corner of the Lever end on the Manchester Road side. I saw a number lads wearing orange boiler suits being attacked from all sides. They came in with the intention of taking the home end but they came unstuck. Fist and kicks were landing on target. They were chased across the Lever end, running for their dear lives. Some had to dive over the fence to escape a certain beating. A few were not so fortunate and got a bad kicking. Some were carried out on stretchers. I saw one guy taken out with a dart stuck in his head. others were lying unconscious and they looked in a bad way. After all the bravado, that was the last time my dad would ever attend a game with me.

Blackpool 1974.

I started to go to more games now, as I was working and I could easily afford to travel the length and breadth of the country. Blackpool would be my first away game and they were our Lancashire rivals. As it turned out it was to be one of the darkest days in football, when sadly, a young Blackpool lad lost his life as he was stabbed to death on the Blackpool kop.

On the morning of the game, I set off with a few lads from Farnworth and we made our way to the train station. On the platform were hundreds of lads all shapes and sizes. Some were skin heads wearing black Crombies (jackets)with white skinners (pants) and Doc Martin boots. There were also mods and punks and after the trouble at the Bolton - Luton game I felt completely safe with them.

The train journey to Blackpool took over an hour and every time we stopped at a train station more lads would jump on. When we finally arrived, the police were waiting for us with dogs. The police couldn't stop the masses of

Bolton fans they just ran straight through them and down the road, in their hundreds. The volume of noise was deafening. All you could hear was, "Bolton are back, Allo, Allo." Shop windows were being kicked in, along the way to the sea front. The only Blackpool fans I saw were in their main pub, The Manchester. All the pub Windows were smashed as the Blackpool fans refused to come out and play.

Inside the ground, we completely filled the away end. There were small pockets of Bolton fans all over the ground. Now and again you would here the chants of, "Bolton aggro," as it kicked off. During the game, you had to dodge bricks and all kinds of missiles being thrown to and fro, from the home end. At half-time, both sets of supporters met up near the cafe at the bottom of the steps and they kicked off, big time. Bolton chased the Blackpool lads back into their end. It was then that a Blackpool lad sadly lost his life. He was stabbed to death. His name was Kevin Olson.

At the end of the game the police held the Bolton fans back. My friends and I were interviewed by the police for over an hour. The police only let us leave two at a time which wasn't good news as there were hundreds of Blackpool lads lying in wait baying for our blood. I was lucky to get back to the train station alive. A lot Bolton fans weren't so lucky as they got picked off one by one and received a good kicking. On the way home, there was a defining silence. I felt sick in the stomach at the thought of young lad being murdered over a game of football. He certainly didn't deserve that. It would be quite a while before I ever set foot inside another football ground.

Manchester United 1974

Ever since I was a young boy I was brought up to hate Manchester United. It had been passed on through generations of my family. It all started in the 1958 cup final at Wembley, when the whole country had sympathy with them after the Munich air disaster. United lost the cup final 2-0 when the great Nat Lofthouse barged Harry Greg and the ball into the back of net. The Bolton team coach was bricked passing through Salford after the United fans took offence after their team was beaten.

So, when this day did arrive against our hated rivals, it was a chance to test us against one of the most feared sets of fans in the country. They had been running amok, up and down the breadth of the country, all season.

On the morning of the match, I was well up for it. We met up with all the Farnworth lads who supported Bolton and we met the Little Hultoners who supported Man United on the flyover bridge between Farnworth and Little Hulton. There were a good 150 of us and we were well outnumbered as there were a good few hundred of them. Everybody was armed to the teeth; sticks bottles, bricks, knives, you name it, they had it. We all waited at the top of the bridge when there was a loud roar and they charged straight into us. They were all wearing Crombies and white skinners with Doc Martins. Quite a few of them had red and white scarves round their hands. I must admit, I shit myself and ran to the back as bricks and bottles rained over all our heads. It was mental. It was man to man fighting. I was attacked by a skinhead who was much older than me. He punched me and knocked me down but I got up and stood my ground which surprised him. He was soon on his toes as I rained a few punches and kicks at him.

Bolton stood their ground. There were casualties on both sides and there were plenty of blooded faces. It was time to scatter as we heard the police sirens in the distance. It was now every man for himself. I and a few others were chased through the long grass but we got away.

I arrived at the game late I was shocked by the sheer numbers of united fans in the away end, it was just a mass of red and white scarves. There must have been 20,000 of them, packed in like sardines. I was in the Lever end with Mick and Frank and there were hundreds of United fans already in there. They had already chased the Bolton lads out of the Lever end and taken the Bolton end. I even saw a lad from my school smiling as he ran past me. He was an ardent United supporter chasing a Bolton lad who was running for his life.

United won the game 1-0 nil. It was a sad day for Bolton in their hooligan history. They had just been run ragged by their most hated rivals.

After the game, I disappeared and I was lucky to get home in one piece.

Millwall 1975

No matter what anybody says about Millwall; they were definitely one of the top firms in the country. They were feared all over and they ran most sets of fans ragged in their own town and in their home end.

Bolton had to get their act together after the humiliation by Manchester United. On the day of the match, we had to improve our organisation and stick together or we would be humiliated once again. On the morning of the game my butterflies were doing double somersaults such was the anticipation and excitement of meeting the Millwall bushwhackers. I arrived in town about midday with Liam, he was mad as a hatter and was fearsome and wasn't afraid of anybody as he proved at Blackpool on our first weekender. Mick and Dave turned out specially for this game. We arrived at the Prince Bill, a well-known haunt where the Bolton lads would meet on a Saturday afternoon on match days. Inside there must have been a good 200 lads.

I looked around and I didn't remember seeing any of their faces at the Bolton Man U game. They never turned up for whatever reason and they probably came up with some good excuses. At about half two, the Millwall train pulled in. We all ran down to meet them. The Millwall lads seemed to be a lot older. Some were in there 40s and they wore white skinners and braces and black Doc Martins which seemed as if they had been polished. Most were skin heads and there were a few rockers. They were surround by police horses and with policeman with dogs.

The Millwall lads tried to run through the police but they were battened back. The odd Bolton lad had a go at them. It was like this all the way to ground just the odd skirmish. I was very impressed with the Millwall lads. They were mental. They only brought a few hundred but every one of them seemed to be crazy. I headed for the Lever end just in time for the kick off. I stuck like glue to Dave knowing that if we were attacked it would take somebody really special, to put him down. It would not be long before I was tested against the mighty Millwall. In the corner of the Lever end there were a good 30 of them. They were huge, all in their 40s and built like brick shit houses. It was like a red rag to a bull. Bolton lads at the Lever end led the attack. Dave was at the forefront of the full-scale attack. The Millwall bushwhackers were getting a good kicking. They started to run towards the fence to jump onto the pitch. Dave was brawling with this huge fella and shouted for me to back him up. I ran straight over and punched him in the side of the head followed by a kick in his shins; it was like a scene from David and Goliath. I was only small and he was huge but I couldn't believe it, I got the better of him. His shirt was ripped and his face was covered in blood as he staggered to the police for protection. The mighty Millwall had been humiliated and they looked a sad sight as they were frogmarched around the pitch to the away end. Most were blooded and limping.

All through the game you would see the odd skirmish as Millwall and Bolton would kick ten bells out of each other. After the game, there were hundreds of Bolton lads lying in wait. They didn't need to wait long as Millwall kicked the gates open only to be met by the hundreds of Bolton lads, baying for their blood. Millwall were legged all the way up Manchester Road to the train station. I saw the odd Millwall bushwhacker stand and have a go but they were soon put on their toes. Bolton had turned the Millwall over and it would go down in legend as one of our biggest scalps. As for me, I was very proud of having had a go at one of the Millwall lads who was twice the size and much older than me. I thanked my dad for toughening me up over the years with all the constant beatings he used to give me.

I would carry on going to football for the next few years meeting up with the lads and getting involved in fights all over the country following my beloved Bolton Wanderers. We faced the likes of Chelsea, Arsenal, Tottenham and Blackburn who I grew to hate with a passion and of course the Scousers with their funny haircuts and their funny accents. I would eventually face the full wrath of the law and be locked up for my troubles. That would become a regular thing but that's another chapter and another story for another time.

Chapter Thirty-Three

Window Cleaner

I was just 15 years old still at school and still getting into mischief; something that still riled my dad no end. I was still very immature for my age. I was also still small in comparison with boys of my own age. (and with no brains as my dad used to remind me every day)

I think my dad had a short memory. I was locked in my room many times through my youth, right or wrongly. I was playing catch up now specially when it came to girls, something I intended to change.

I remember coming home from school late as usual and blooded after another fight with our local Saint James school pupils. I still didn't have a key to get into the house something which used to upset me a lot, especially when most of my mates had their own keys.

I knocked on the door and my dad opened it. I was half expecting a smack across the face or a rabbit punch; something which he became an expert with over the years.

He told me to come in the front room as he wanted a chat with me. I followed my dad and he just said, "Sit thee down lad. As you know I haven't been working lately. Money is short and we can't keep relying on your mother's money."

I just looked puzzled and I thought to myself, 'what the hell has that got to do with me?"

Before I could get a word in edgeways he dropped a bombshell. He said, "Well lad, at the weekends you will be working for a friend of mine, window cleaning."

"Window cleaning," I stuttered. "I don't like heights for God's sake. Dad."

He started to get agitated and I was half expecting a dig at any moment. I was on my own with him. My mum wasn't there as she was working on Bolton market so I couldn't ask her to get me out of the situation I was in.

My dad just grabbed my hair and slapped me across the face and told me to shut up and listen to what he had to say. He just came straight out with it. "You start work on Saturday morning with Joe and you will do it if you like it or not. Do you understand Ian?"

Before I could reply with an answer he slapped me again across the face. I pleaded with him to stop as he was hurting me. I ran upstairs into my room and just lay on my bed crying.

Saturday arrived very quickly and Joe came to my house to pick me up. It was 9.30 in the morning. It was dull and wet and my dad kept out the way as he usually did when my face was marked. This used to irritate me as everybody liked him and they were oblivious to what was going on with all the abuse. Anyway, I heard a knock on the door, it was Joe. He was quite small with a lot of stubble around his face, quite tubby and he looked in his sixties. The first thing he said to me was, what was I like with heights?

I just laughed and replied, "I don't like heights."

Joe just laughed and said, "Don't worry Ian, you will be fine. You will soon get used to it."

For the first few days I was on the Bird estate which was near my house. At the beginning, I was just carrying the ladders and filling his buckets up with warm soapy water. After a few days training he showed me how to clean a bottom window then he watched me clean another one. I found it very difficult at first. The windows were full of streaks. Joe kept repeating to me to ring my leather or Chammy out. I was leaving too much soapy water on the leather. The Chammy had to be damp or the Windows wouldn't be properly clean. I didn't wear any gloves and after a while I would lose the feeling in my hands it was that cold and that was in the first hour.

I watched Joe climb up the ladder with ease, cleaning the top windows. After he cleaned the house front and back it was my turn. I was petrified, my fear of heights was stronger than ever. I had to do it as I had no choice. I had to earn some money for my dad or face his wrath. I was determined to beat my fears and win the fight. Something I had learned with my dad after it was beaten into me by him.

At first I used to cling on to the ladder for dear life to the amusement of Joe who used to laugh his socks off. At first, I didn't wear a bib to hold the Chammy. I used to take the bucket of soapy water up the ladder and at the same time try to clean the Windows. I did drop the bucket a few times and soak Joe but he took it all in good humour. After several attempts, I did improve. I wasn't perfect but I was getting there.

I still had a few hiccups which had Joe in hysterics. The number of times he told me to leave the bucket on the floor and climb up the ladder with a wet Chammy in one hand and the dry cleaning Chammy in the other hand and whilst climbing up the ladder the water would run down inside my jacket sleeve wetting my arm and adding to my discomfort. By the time I reached the second house, the water in the bucket was now cold.

Joe came over and told me, "Come on Ian, we haven't got all day. Your bucket needs filling with warm water. Go and call at the house with the red door. She's very obliging," Joe said with a big smile. I could swear there was ice in the bucket and it was early autumn, that's how cold it felt. Anyway, I knocked on the red door and a woman with blonde hair in her late twenties answered. She was wearing a thin white nightie that didn't leave much to your imagination. I could see straight through her nightie and I could clearly see that she had ample breasts. I was clearly in awe of her.

She spoke to me in a soft voice. "What can I do for you love?"

I replied Joe said that you would fill my bucket up with warm water."

With a big smile on her face she said, "Come in love, I will put the kettle on."

I followed her in and she told me her name was Mary and asked me what my name was.

"Ian," I muttered with a nervous voice.

Mary put the kettle on the stove then turned around and started to unbutton her white nightie and said, "Come on love, you have only got till the kettle boils." I stood there frozen for a few seconds and in complete silence I could not believe what was happening. She came over and started to unzip my trousers I was shitting myself. For a split-second I thought, it was all set up by Joe.

She muttered in my left ear and said, "You are not shy Ian, are you?"

I was already standing to attention. She pulled my trousers down then pushed me onto the kitchen table. She then climbed on top of me and we started to have sex. She moaned and said, "Slow down Ian, it will be better for the both of us."

I started to a do a long slow rhythm which I must admit was very sensual and by the sound of her moans she was enjoying it. I then got carried away. I climbed on top of her and I set off like a rocket. We were like rabbits, we couldn't get enough of each other. I must have climaxed at least three times which was a first for me. After a few minutes the kettle boiled. I could tell as it was whistling. This didn't make any difference to Mary, she just carried on. She was moving faster than I was. She was like an electric train. She was biting my lips and pulling my hair which didn't go down well with me as I am hair sore. She then pushed me off, smiled at me and then pleasured me. We then kissed each other for a few seconds and just got dressed. The sex was amazing I had never experienced anything like that before. It was just fantastic, she was so experienced.

Mary then filled my bucket and with a large grin on her face, whispered, "Call any time if you want your bucket filled." She gave me a small peck on my cheek opened the door and said, "See you love, till the next time."

Joe was waiting across the road. I could see a big grin on his face and he muttered, "Did you have a good time Ian?"

I just smiled and nodded my head.

He just said, with a loud laugh "Mary has a fetish for young boys and I hope you enjoyed one of the perks of the job." He then said, with a chuckle, "Anyway come on Ian, we are behind now, I hope you are not too tired to carry on."

I couldn't believe what happened. Most women on the round would just give me a cup of tea and biscuits but Mary was something quite different.

As days passed by, I would see some sights. Various women in a state of undress while I was cleaning their windows and they knew I was watching but I just classed it as a perk of the job.

After my first week Joe give me my first wage packet. It was £10 but I never saw any of it as my dad took it all.

I worked for Joe for 6 months in all kinds of inclement weather. The sex sessions would carry on with Mary so that more than compensated for that.

It would all come to an end as Joe died suddenly. He had heart trouble, so I was told. I will always have fond memories of working for Joe, his witty humour and his kindness and the guidance he gave me for which I was truly grateful.

R.I.P Joe I will never forget you.

Chapter Thirty-Four

Tables are Finally Turned

After years of inflicting abuse on me and my mother, I started to fight back against my father. Protecting my mother became the hardest challenge. She had suffered physical and mental torture for most of her married life. She always protected the family, lied about the beatings and the abuse to protect the family name.

All this would finally come to an end. I was sixteen years old and had just started work at William Walkers in Bolton. I was still getting the odd punch and facing his constant abuse and he was still treating my mother like dirt, on the odd occasion. He would be brave and chase my mother up Derwent Road in full view of prying eyes.

People were starting to ask questions about the screams in our house and the constant bruises on our faces. My mum tried her best to cover them with make- up but to no avail, as word had got around about my dad's abuse. It certainly wasn't me who told on him, I was too afraid. Maybe my mum had trusted someone and they had passed it around. We never found out who started the talk.

Whenever we went out shopping, people at the shops would point at us and they would always come over and say, "Are you are alright with a caring smile."

My dad had totally lost it by now. He was either getting braver or he was finally losing his marbles. His drinking had become worse and he started to leave empty bottles of sherry all over the house. He didn't care who was listening. He didn't try to hide his anger in front of the neighbours or anybody else for that matter which made him a more dangerous animal.

From the age of fourteen, I started to fight back with him to stop him beating me and to protect my mother. Of course, he always got the better of me and would punish me for trying to stand up to him. I lost count of the times he twisted my arm up my back or banged my head on the wall but all this would come to an end.

And the tables would finally be turned against my father who had over so many years physically abused and tormented the family; so much so that we all lived a life of fear.

I was sixteen years old. I was a young and immature but a tough little cookie who started to be able to defend himself.

On this day, as usual, I got up a bit late for my breakfast. I was finding it very difficult to get up at six in the morning and starting work at 7.30am. My mum made me egg on toast or sometimes I would get a treat, bacon and eggs with fried bread and tomatoes. This was usually on a Friday as it was my pay day. I was talking to my mum in the doorway when my dad came and slammed the door on my fingers. I yelped out in pain but he just burst out laughing. My mum had a real go at him but he just laughed it off. I went upstairs and put my fingers under the cold water to try and numb the pain. I was in agony. I wanted to kill him but I didn't have the guts. He was waiting for a reaction but I didn't fall for the bait. I walked up Derwent Road seething and in pain. It was a long day at work. I was in complete agony. I ended up seeing the first-aider who bandaged my three badly swollen fingers.

The day passed I went home and my dad wasn't in. He was at the bookies, gambling no doubt. It was my wage but, unbeknown to him, I used to give my mum some of my spending money.

I chatted a lot to my mum as I was getting older. Gradually she would tell me things about my dad's dark past, like telling me the number of times he was in prison and all the women he used to knock about with and of the times he used to beat her, even before I was born. I truly hated him for all the things he did, especially to my mum who I worshipped. Gone were the days I would come out in a nervous rash, soil my pants or wet my bed or cry on my school desk. Those day were over. I was older and more street-wise and I could handle myself a lot better.

It would be around 7.30 in the evening. He came home late. I could feel the tension in the house. I looked at my mum's face. I could see that she was getting very nervous. It was obvious now he had gone for a drink and that he would be drunk when he got home.

The knock on the door was the sign of his arrival. I was sitting on the chair watching TV. I could hear my dad staggering in at the door and having a go at my mum, for nothing as usual. He then went straight to the TV and turned the channel over, much to my annoyance.

I told him gently, "I'm watching that dad."

He threw a punch at me which caught my lip. This was my chance. I knew he was drunk. I jumped up in anger and lost count of the number of times I punched him in the face. I was oblivious to the pain in my fingers such was the anger I was in. My dad was totally shocked he tried to stagger away but such was my anger that I carried on beating him. I just couldn't stop. I held him in an arm lock and I carried on hitting him in the face. He was screaming for me to stop. I think I would have killed him but for the intervention of my mum. I threw him on the floor and I screamed at him and called him a coward. "Get up and fight me, I shouted."

He wouldn't fight back, he was too frightened.

My mum put a five pound note in my hand and told me to calm down and go for a drink.

Before I went out, I put my foot in his face and said, "That's for all the hurt you have caused me and my mum over the years." I walked out and went for a drink in the Flying Shuttle until the early hours. Eventually, I decided it was time to go home. I tried the front door. It was locked. For a moment, I thought I had been kicked out or my dad was seriously hurt. I went around the back of the house and I saw the kitchen light on. I saw my dad look through the window at me. He appeared to be in bad way. His face was black and blue. Both his eyes were shutting and his right cheek was badly swollen. I must admit, for a split second, I actually felt sorry for him.

He opened the door and said, "Are you coming in or not?"

I casually walked past him expecting a slap across my head but it never happened. He was now a broken man, a forlorn shadow of his former self.

A few days later, after I came home from work, I opened the kitchen door and there he was. His head was in the oven. He said he was trying to kill himself but I didn't believe him for one minute. I shouted at him to get his head out of the oven and stop looking for attention.

I told him, "Next time, make sure you turn the gas on." I muttered to myself as I walked away, "you should have done that years ago."

My father was never the same again. He had lost total control over me and he couldn't handle it. His was now an alcoholic, it was the only way he could deal with it. He never touched my mum again, or me for that matter. The tables had finally been turned and it was all of his own making.

Chapter Thirty-Five

Blighty's

Blighty's was a night club in Farnworth which was located on Church Street, just off Market Street, facing the old police station. It was a night club loved by all, not just the Farnworth and Bolton people but people from all over the north west. Blighty's had two floors.

Downstairs was a large dance floor with a removable stage and chairs all around the dance floor. In the corner was a small buffet, On Thursdays they used to do a special deal where you could get chicken and chips on 'grab a granny night' and it was only 20p a shot, which went down well with the locals.

Upstairs you had two dance floors with two discos. In the 1960s and 70s, the club featured many top line acts. Alvin Stardust, Showwaddy, Slade, the Drifters, and Tommy

Cooper (who was always drunk on stage, or so I was told) Frankie Laine, Jerry Lee Lewis to name a few. Coaches used to come from all over the north west, although Friday nights were sometimes disrupted as our friends from Liverpool came along to enjoy the taste of their own blood.

Blighty's was transformed every weekend. Every Friday and Saturday night, the place was over capacity, rammed jammed and crammed to the rafters. There were always plenty of girls to choose from.

The atmosphere was fuelled by alcohol and the bars always did great business. It was the best place in Bolton.

It had a strict dress code, you were only let in if you were wearing a shirt and tie. The idea was to keep out the riff-raff (the assumption was that riff raff, scruffy sods, didn't dress very well.)

In 1974 I was just sixteen. It was at that time that I started to frequent the place. At the time, I was working so I had money to buy the clothes and the drink and generally have a good time. I didn't always get in to Blighty's. My mates always looked older than me. Most of them had stubble. I was lucky to have any at all. There was a certain bouncer who used to watch out for me and when he saw me he always refused me entrance. He used to give me a smack round the head and tell me, with a smirk on his face, to go home as it was passed my bedtime and my mummy would be waiting for me. I was too scared to give him any backchat as he was built like a brick shit house, one punch from him and I wouldn't have seen Christmas Day.

I always met up with a few lads from Highfield; Frank, Liam, Gez to a name a few. We usually had a few beers in either Queens, The Post Office, Smokies or The Black Horse on Market Street and then we would make our way to Blighty's. We always made sure we didn't look too pissed (drunk)and we would all make sure our ties were straight. That was a headache for me as it was always a struggle to try to get my knot right on my tie, even in my school days.

I eventually found it easier to gain entrance to the night club after the bouncer had left for some reason. On the odd occasion, I did get stopped as they said I was too drunk. They didn't know that I had only had 3 pints of beer but I couldn't take my drink

I remember meeting one girl from Kearsley. I think she was called Bev. She was about 16 years old but looked a lot older with long brown hair and huge breasts which you couldn't miss, as her low-cut dress plunged so much that you could see her belly button.

After dancing to The Drifters, I took her to the bar and bought her a vodka and coke. She smiled with a big grin and said, "Don't think you are going to get me drunk, so you can get your leg over."

I just raised my eye-brows with a canny smile".

By the end of the night she was slightly drunk. I took her on the car park behind the club which wasn't well lit up and before we knew it our lips were locked and her tongue was in and out of my mouth like an electric drill. She unzipped my pants and then slid her hand down and grabbed my penis. Then, before I knew what was happening, my pants were round my ankles and she had me pressed me against the wall. Then she lifted her dress up and we had sex. It only lasted a few minutes as we got interrupted by another pub goer. I was glad really, I was bloody knackered. Bev was like a dog on heat, pardon the pun.

Before I walked back into club, I said my goodbyes. I left my usual mark on her neck which we called a luv bite. It was the usual gift from me. It was like a trophy, another bed notch as people used to say. My legs were like jelly as I walked back into the club through the back exit, like a bloody cowboy.

And talking about Cowboys, it was like the Wild West on some Friday nights. Coaches used to come from all over the north west, especially Liverpool. They all had funny haircuts and accents we used to call them the Beatle boys, good with their mouths but nothing else. They tried to take over the dance floor with their stupid dance routines.

Now and again a few pint-pots would land on the dance floor from some of our local nutters who didn't take too kindly to them chatting up our women. and trying to take over the place. The odd fight would start and then it would turn into one mass brawl. This happened every Friday night for months on end.

After a few of local lads got stabbed and glassed, a lot of the locals wanted total revenge. Bolton and the Farnworth lads were predominately Bolton Wanderers fans. We all knew each other, so we always stuck together.

One certain Friday night, we were all on Church Street, waiting for the Liverpool coaches to park on the club's car park. There must have been over 200 lads. Some of the biggest nutters from Farnworth, Little lever and Bolton were there including myself, Frank, Gez, Mick, Dave, Liam and Tez. We were all waiting with excitement on the road side next to the car park.

Then one of the local lads came running down the road shouting and screaming, "The Liverpool lads are here. There are two coaches of the fuckers."

The coaches had to pass us to get on to the Car park and soon as they did all hell broke out. The coaches' windows were put through with bricks and sticks and the odd iron bar and a hammer was used. You could hear the Liverpool lads screaming. Some were covered in blood and cowering behind the coach seats. There was no escape for them as our lads surrounded the coaches. The drivers were hiding behind the seats, so, the coaches weren't going anywhere. This carried on for a good five minutes which seemed like an eternity at the time, before the police came. Me and my mates decided to do a runner and cut through all the back streets as we headed to Highfield where we all lived.

We decided to give Blighty's a miss that night as we all knew the police would be looking for the culprits. The following day word got around that a couple of the Liverpool lads had been stabbed after one of the coach doors had been ripped off. As far as I knew, I never heard of anybody being arrested for the incident.

It would be a couple of weeks before we all ventured back in to Blighty's. You still saw the odd Liverpool lad but they were a different crowd that came now to Blighty's. They came with their girl-friends so that was that, with them.

I still got into the odd fight with a few outsiders. I was hardened and experienced now after the hidings I used to get and not just from my father, being involved in the gangs and football violence at Burnden Park the home of my beloved Bolton Wanderers, so I could handle myself now which came in handy in Farnworth. It was a rough place to live in, at that time so you had to stand up for yourself.

Now and again our football allegiances would be tested as coaches started to come from Burnley, Manchester and Blackburn who I hated with a passion, after being arrested in 1973 and punished in a juvenile court when I was just 15 years old.

I got my revenge at the disco-bar upstairs. This Blackburn lad was showing off in front of his mates, slagging off a girl who I was treating. It wasn't that that upset me, he was slagging off Bolton wanderers. I just head butted him which probably hurt me more than it did him but he went down like he had been shot and that's was that. His mates just walked away, all six of them and they didn't do a thing to help him. It was now 2.30 in the morning. Frank and I decided to leave. As we walked on the car park, I could see my Blackburn friend who I had head-butted early. He wasn't alone. There was a full coach of them and they ran straight into us. We were both kicked all over the car park.

With all the shouting and all the commotion that was going on, the local lads came to our rescue and chased the Blackburn lads off. A couple of them were badly beaten as Frank and I were but we just laughed it off as one of those things. Some you win, some you lose, as the saying went.

Back to the girls. I danced and drank with girls from all over the north west and had sex with a lot of them. I lost count after so many but I didn't always get my own way. I was smacked a few times, drinks thrown over me but it was all part of the territory so it didn't bother me in the slightest

One girl that did stand out was Shirley from Blackburn. Yes, she was from Blackburn but she had a pair of tits and blonde hair so it didn't matter to me where she came from. Anyway, Shirley was as fit as a butcher's dog, as they used to say where I lived in Highfield. She was absolutely gorgeous. She had long blonde hair with a white low top showing off her breasts and tight blue jeans with long black boots on which didn't do my blood pressure any good. I wasn't my usual self, a cocky little shit. I was the very opposite, shy, polite, it was as though she had put some kind of spell on me. It would be a couple of hours before we kissed and that was just a couple pecks on the dance floor. I did my usual embarrassing act. I slipped on the dance floor and knocked a girl over and ruined her pink top with her drink which was a vodka and Vimto. Thankfully she took it in good part which was a relief. Shirley thought it was funny and she giggled for most of the night. At the end of the night I asked how she was getting home.

She replied that she came in her car so it didn't matter what time she got back, which put a huge smile on my face. We both left the club I said my good byes to Mick and Frank winked at them both and smiled and said see you later. We walked hand in hand to her car which was parked on a side street just off Market Street. Along the way, we had a few cuddles and gropes so I was already worked up when we reached her car. She had a white old Volkswagen Beetle. Inside she had leather seats with pink covers. We both got in and she drove off and she took me to a place called Darwin which is just outside of Blackburn. She parked down a country lane and then stopped, turned the lights out, opened the door and pushed the leather seats back then got in the back. We just started kissing each other slowly. I looked at her white top. I could see her breasts bulging out of her white bra. It wasn't long before that was off and everything else. She did the same to me and we were both naked. She then kissed me slowly down my stomach then put her hand on my crotch, then she pleasured me. I was tingling all over. She then climbed on top of me and we had sex. We did it three times and in different positions. It was a fantastic and sensual experience. She later dropped me off at the top of my road. We kissed and cuddled and then said our goodbyes after saying we would see each other next week. We didn't, which was a massive disappointment to me as I was very keen on her.

I carried on going to Blighty's. I did meet a couple more girls but it didn't mean anything to me, not like it did with Shirley.

I still got in the odd scuffle with lads from out-of-town or for upsetting some lads when I was chatting with their girl-friends.

I stopped going to Blighty's in the 80s when the club changed its name to City Lights. I felt the club had lost its identity.

I have fond memories of Blighty's. I saw some great acts like Shawwaddy and The Drifters, danced to some great music. Heard some fantastic Abba tunes and had some fun with the Liverpool lads (Beatle boys) and finally the girls. Who could forget Shirley. I never did. Some great memories and good times.

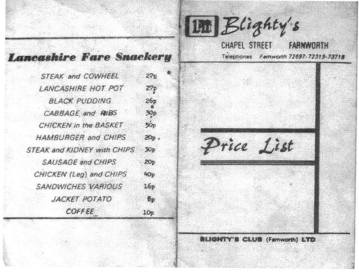

Blighty's

CHAPEL STREET   FARNWORTH
Telephones   Farnworth 72697-72319-73718

Lancashire Fare Snackery

STEAK and COWHEEL	27p
LANCASHIRE HOT POT	27p
BLACK PUDDING	26p
CABBAGE and RIBS	30p
CHICKEN in the BASKET	50p
HAMBURGER and CHIPS	20p
STEAK and KIDNEY with CHIPS	30p
SAUSAGE and CHIPS	20p
CHICKEN (Leg) and CHIPS	40p
SANDWICHES VARIOUS	16p
JACKET POTATO	8p
COFFEE	10p

Price List

BLIGHTY'S CLUB (Farnworth) LTD

Chapter Thirty-Six

Wigan Casino

Around about the year 1974 I started to venture out of Farnworth I was bored with the clubs and bars where I lived. I wanted to go somewhere different. I wanted a bit more excitement. The world was my oyster. The days when I was in my father's shackles, had disappeared forever. They had fallen by the wayside even though I was still living at home. My mum was more settled and my father wouldn't say a boo to a goose.

I wasn't particularly into any music, but I did have a soft spot for Abba. I had already frequented the likes of the Nevada and Blighty's and most of the bars. I enjoyed the music and the odd scuffle but the girls were my main intentions. I was working so I had money, for the first time in my life, so hitting the night clubs and bars wasn't a problem. While I was at the football I got talking to some Wigan lads who followed Bolton Wanderers. We talked about night clubs and bars and during the conversation Wigan casino was mentioned. He said the club stayed open all night, it was non-alcoholic.

"But you had a good drink before you went in. The music was top class and so were the women. They came from all over the north west," he told me.

That was enough to get my attention.

A few others and I decided to try it. It would be a few weeks before we frequented the place. There were clubs for purists, for innovators, for collectors, but if what you really wanted was a club for dancers, then Wigan Casino was the place to be. Young people from all over the UK regularly made the trek to Wigan Casino to hear the latest Northern

Soul artists and to dance. Queues to get in were sometimes five or six people deep, and stretched around the corner up into the town centre.

The second dance floor, called Mr. M's, stayed open until 6.00 am and played oldies songs from a variety of DJs. Every all-nighter traditionally ended with three songs that became known as the *3 before 8*: *Time Will Pass You By,* by Tobi Legend, *Long After Tonight Is Over* by Jimmy Radcliffe, and *I'm On My Way* by Dean Parrish. Parrish is still active on the Northern Soul circuit.

It was a Friday night when we first visited the place. There were five of us, from Farnworth, all good lads and fun to be with. Mick, Ged, Frank and Liam. We went everywhere together, Blighty's, The Nevada. We shared the same drinks. If one of us was skint, in the early days, we even shared the same girls, just for a laugh. We caught the late bus to Wigan. We were already tipsy from our earlier visits to Smokies and Queens on Market Street in Farnworth. The bus ride took over an hour. We seemed to be stopping at every stop, picking people up. A lot of them had badges sewn on their jumpers and pants with the name of Wigan Casino all over them.

We finally arrived in Wigan and headed for the town centre. A lot of the bars were already packed and we couldn't get into a lot of them. We found a bar down a side street. There were plenty of people standing outside drinking and there was girl who couldn't keep her eyes of me. I just smiled and winked, like you do. Then we casually walked into the bar. Ged got a round in. "A Vodka and Coke," I shouted, "with ice." We collected our drinks and went outside. I looked around to see if I could still see the blonde piece but she had already gone.

We stayed for a couple of hours then headed for Station Road where Wigan Casino was. Outside the building the queues were massive. It was unbelievable, the volume of people, I had never see anything like it.

Walking through the doors at the top of the stairs, after paying to get in we were hit by a wall of heat, the smell of men's Brut and sweat.

Seeing my reflection in the mirror wrapped around the post as you walked past toward the dance floor, getting showered by nicotine stained drops of condensation, feeling the hair on the back of your neck stand up, I was buzzing. People were dancing on the dance floor like there was no tomorrow. It truly was an unbelievable sight. The dance-floor was huge. There were thousands of people dancing; spinning youths throwing themselves round the dance-floor in 32-inch wide spenders (pants) and vests adorned with the badges of their favourite 'nighters.' Slogans like, *Keep the Faith, Heart of Soul,* and *The Night Owl.*

We climbed up the stairs and leaned over the balcony with our jaws dropping at the packed floor where sounds like Rhino, Tomangoes and the Vel-Vets were to be heard. We spoke to people from all over the country, Wolverhampton, London, Stoke and far afield as Aberdeen. Drug abuse was rife. I got propositioned in the men's toilets. He was pedalling Amphetamine. I told him to do one as I don't do drugs. I felt like dropping him such was the arrogance of the lad. If he had told me he was from Blackburn I would have done, such was the hatred I had for them.

I had to laugh. Gez and Frank tried to copy some of the dancers on the floor. They seemed to get their legs tangled and fell over. I couldn't stop laughing, it was so funny. There was no way I was attempting it, not with my track record on the dance floor. I had made a fool of myself too often.

You could hear the odd Motown tracks bellowing in the back ground but you guessed there weren't too many from the Supremes. And if there were, I reckon, I would have known them. It was at the entrance that it seemed the best dancers were given extra room. I remember this guy in a blue and green striped shirt, a black guy and he looked like Arthur Ash, you know the famous tennis player. He was with a brilliant girl dancer; they seemed to own the place, they were so good.

I looked around the place and it seemed like a bit of a dump. The toilets were stinky and sweaty but the old place had character. We decide to go for a mooch (walk around) and in the corner of my eye, you guessed it, I saw the blonde girl. She was with three other girls. One of them was a very fat girl, she was so fat that you could see the flab hanging over her pants and her breasts were huge.

"I always like big boobs but I think I'll pass on this one," I said to Frank. "She's all yours as you like fat birds."

I started chatting to the blond piece whose name was Cindy. She was wearing a short blue dress with gold sequins, (evening dress) her blonde hair was quite long and half way down her back. Her breasts looked quite ample but what stood out to me was her bright red lips and her luscious smile. It wouldn't take long before I had sampled them. Cindy was from Burnley and we got on quite well throughout the night. Cindy was quite an experienced dancer as she had been coming for over seven months. I watched her dance on the dance floor and she was amazing. The way she moved her legs and threw herself around the floor doing her spins, used to make me sick in the stomach.

I tried a little myself, trying to copy Cindy but my legs used to get in a tangle and I would end up on the floor, much to Cindy's amusement.

I could help myself laughing at Frank with the fat bird, she was crushing him against the balcony. She was like a praying mantis trying to get her tongue down Franks throat.

The night seemed to go very quickly. It was nearly Six in the morning and time to go. I was hoping I could get a few minutes with Cindy before she caught the coach home. I would have been disappointed if I missed out on her. We went for a short walk and we went down a side street. I pressed her against the wall and we started kissing. My hands were all over her. Cindy responded by unzipping my pants and slowly put her hand towards my crotch. It didn't take long for me to get erect. As she put her tongue in my mouth, I nearly exploded all over her dress as she pleasured me and it was over before it started. Then who came walking around the corner, bloody Frank with his praying mantis (fat bird)? I could have killed him. So, that was that. Who knows what would have happened with Cindy? I'll leave that to your imagination.

I left Frank to his own devices with the fat bird I didn't fancy watching them put on a show. I told them I would meet them outside Wigan casino with the rest of the gang.

I had a few pecks on the way back with Cindy and I couldn't resist feeling her breasts now and again on the way back. I said my goodbyes to Cindy and her friends and that would be the last time I would see them.

I met up with the rest of my Farnworth clan, Mick, Ged and Liam and went to look for Frank and his fat bird. We caught them at it. Frank had his pants down giving what for to this huge fat bird, it was not a pleasant sight, I could tell thee. But Frank was Frank, it was another notch on his bed post bless him.

We frequented Wigan casino a few more times, not for the dancing at which I was useless, but to sample the atmosphere; the music which was played mostly on an archaic sound system, the chewing gum on the floor, condensation/nicotine marks on your clothes next morning During the summer nights, you had to go out for a breather but when you went back in, it was like an oven. I was in total awe of the place, the crowd and the friends I made, are all part of happy memories. I loved the whole place, the people, the dancers, the music, the heat. Returned numerous times but now regret not going more regularly. Still I feel privileged to be able to say, I was there. If you told people you spent all night in a club with no alcohol, and girls and boys didn't dance together they thought you were mad!

Saw Junior Walker and Martha Reeves - both were brilliant. Seem to remember Martha doing 'One Way Out' with no musical backing. Both were brilliant.

These were fantastic memories, and of course our Cindy. It was a total pleasure meeting her. It was short and sweet but well worth it.

Chapter Thirty-Seven

Who Am I

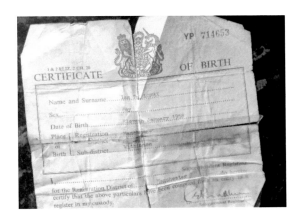

At the age of 17 I found out some information which would totally shock me to the very core and affect my life for ever.

The year was 1975. I was working at the time at William Walkers, a tannery in Bolton. I was on good money. Silvia and I had decided to go on a holiday together. My mum and dad agreed as they quite liked her. Mum was happy at the idea of me settling down after all the troubles I had been getting myself into. I had been courting Silvia for a few months now which was a world record for me. Silvia was the same age as me and had long beautiful blonde curly hair with blue eyes. She was quite petite and very attractive, (well I would say that wouldn't I.) She was as mad as a hatter at school. Silvia didn't just fight the girls, she would end up fighting the boys.

It was my day off work and I planned to go to the births and marriages building in Bolton for a birth certificate so I could then get a passport for my holiday. I got up in a very good mood and I was very happy that I was going abroad. I was whistling which was very unusual in my house. I sat down at the table having my breakfast, scrambled eggs on toast followed by fresh orange juice which I always bought myself, as my mum said it was too expensive for her to buy. My dad asked me why I was in such a good mood.

I replied, "I'm going to get my passport so I can go on holiday with Silvia." He was quiet and not very responsive which was just him anyway. I looked at my mum and she was not her usual self either. I never thought anything of it at the time but looking back I understood why they both looked so glum.

I kissed my mum like I always did and headed up Derwent Road to the bus stop. On my way, I bumped into Frank and he asked me why I was in such a good mood.

I replied, "I'm going to get a passport as I'm going to go on holiday with my girlfriend."

The bus to Bolton was late as usual, something which always irritated me. I decided to walk across the town centre and look at the holidays in the travel shops.

I looked at quite a few holidays in the windows and this particular holiday stood out for me. It was a four-day trip to Amsterdam.

I headed for the births and marriages building which was on Le Mans Crescent facing the police station, a place I would get accustomed to over the years. I had to go up to the second floor. It was a large office and you had to go to a window to been seen to. There was a large queue. I couldn't sit down as all the seats had been taken so I had to wait my turn standing. It would take me over an hour before I could actually see somebody. Eventually my turn came and I asked the lady in question, a blonde-haired woman with spectacles who spoke with a Scouse accent which I couldn't understand, for a birth certificate. I remember thinking to myself, 'Why don't they speak the bloody Queen's English.'

She replied, "Write your name and details on this form."

I wrote my name, "Ian Minihane, my age and address."

She smiled and said, "Please sit down and I will call you over when I am ready."

It would be a good twenty minutes before she finally shouted my name and said to me, "I have checked the details you gave me and your name doesn't exist. "Are you sure you have given me the right details?"

I replied, "Yes, I have. Could you go and check again please as I need the birth certificate for my passport."

She went away and it wasn't long before she came back with the same answer, "I have checked and double checked the details you have given me. They are incorrect and this person doesn't exist."

I was gobsmacked (shocked). I walked away without saying another word. My mind was working overtime. I just didn't know what to think. I started to worry and was getting quite emotional and then anger started to set in. I walked across the town centre in a robotic mode. I didn't even notice people passing me by, such was the utter shock.

I headed straight for the off-licence on Newport Street for a few cans of beer as I always did when I got upset. That, of course, was something I used to do a lot in my younger days because of the constant abuse from my father. I headed for Bradford Road which was on the way to my house. It was there that I sat down on a bench and drank four cans of beer. I didn't know what I was feeling but I knew I was very angry. I just couldn't fathom (think) what was going on. It only took me four beers before I was a bit tipsy. I headed straight to my house with a severe headache, not just because of the beer but because of the anger. I could feel the blood flowing through my body.

What normally was a thirty-minute walk home, took me over an hour and half. When I finally arrived at my house, I knocked on the front door and my mum answered. I just ignored her and headed straight into the front room where I saw my dad who was sitting on the couch reading the newspaper. I just came straight out with it. "Who am I dad?" I said. "I just tried to get a bloody birth certificate and they told me my name doesn't exist.

He nervously said, "Sit thee down, lad." He then muttered nervously, "I have been dreading this day for a very long time." He then continued, "You are not called Minihane. Your name is Lomax."

I replied, "What you talking about? When I met your mother, I was still married and your mother became pregnant with my baby. It was because of that, we moved to Didsbury because I didn't want anybody to find out about us. So, when you were born, I registered your name as Lomax, the same name as me and your mother, as though we were a normal family. I had to," my father replied. "In them days, it was a disgrace for a married man to have an affair. That's why we moved away and I lied to your mother and told her I was called Lomax because I didn't want to lose her as I loved her."

"How you can you say you loved her after lying to her?" I saw red I just laid in to him. I punched him silly and knocked him off his chair it was then I grabbed a large picture off the wall and hit him over the head with it. Such was the anger, I didn't realise he was covered in blood and cowering like the coward he was. It only lasted minutes but he was badly hurt and lay motionless on the floor.

My mum come running into the room screaming, "You have killed him, Ian."

I just replied, "I don't care. I hate him for what he has done to me over the years."

I just stormed out of the house and went for a walk for hours, not realising that I had walked into Bolton and sat on the benches in the centre, just looking into thin air. I was heartbroken. I started to wonder if he was my real father (which I couldn't give a damn about) and were they all my real brothers and sisters? Was she my real mum? All kinds of things were running in my head. The anger had turned to upset and I couldn't stop crying.

Eventually, I decided to face the music. After beating up my father I didn't know if I had put him in hospital or if I had killed him, such was the venom in side of me? I headed back home but not before I smashed up a phone box, cutting my hand in the process but I didn't care or even feel it, although I was bleeding profusely which needed stitches later on. I nervously knocked on the front door and my mum answered it and took me in to the front room.

"Ian," she said, "I am your mother, you know that. Look in the mirror at yourself, you can see me. He's your dad and they are your real brothers and sisters. I honestly didn't know he was married. As for Lomax, I didn't know till years later and that's the truth, on your life," she replied.

I held my mum in my arms and cried a thousand tears. I didn't care if he wasn't my dad, I just couldn't handle it if she was not my mother.

I calmed down and I worriedly asked my mum, "How's my dad?"

She replied, "He has a black eye and his face is badly swollen and he has a sore head." Then she smiled and said, "Its only what he deserves for what he's done over the years to our family." She told me to keep away from him till it blew over.

It would be weeks before I ever spoke to him again. He never said he was sorry and I never mentioned Lomax to him. I spoke to my sisters and brothers and they were in utter shock but they always reminded me that I was their brother and that they loved me.

All those years I thought I was called Ian Minihane from birth. Everybody knew me as Minihane hence the nick name 'Mini.' It did affect me badly but I started to get used to the name.

As for my holiday, I did eventually go on holiday with Silvia to Amsterdam and that would be another story.

Chapter Thirty-eight

Amsterdam

After the trouble I had had with my dad about the Lomax debacle, I decided to go to Amsterdam for a few days. My mum was fine about it even though I was under 18.

First of all, I needed to get a passport and I knew it would take a few weeks. Silvia's parents had given her permission so it was ok on that score. I intended to go to the passport office for the documents and then book the holiday for Amsterdam in the morning.

I got up early and my mum was already downstairs in the kitchen. "Do you want some cheese on toast Ian?"

I replied that will be fine thanks, mum."

I looked in the front room and I couldn't see my dad, about so I asked my mum where he was.

"In bed," she replied. It was obvious now he was avoiding me and to tell you the truth I didn't particularly care.

I sat down at the table eating my cheese on toast and my mum put her head through the door. "Do you want your birth certificate, Ian?"

I turned around and smiled and said, "Please mum."

She put my birth certificate in front of me on the table and then went out of the room and shut the door. I studied my birth certificate carefully. I felt very nervous. The butterflies in my stomach were doing summersaults. It would be the very first time that I had set my eyes on it.

I looked closely and there it was my name, *Ian Paul Lomax born in 1958 in Withington Hospital, Didsbury, Manchester.* It started to hit home now. I finally knew who I really was.

Tears started to roll down my face and I just broke down sobbing. My whole upbringing had just been wiped out. Minihane never existed. My father was pure evil.

He totally destroyed my life and my mother's too. He lied to me and my mother. I have no feelings for him now. He has totally destroyed them. How could he keep this a secret without me ever finding out?

My thoughts turned to my mother. She didn't just suffer at his hand but also from his lies. I picked myself up and went into the kitchen and was smoking a cigarette nervously. She turned to me and just smiled. I went over to her and kissed her and I held her in my arms and I whispered down her ear, "Mum, I love you so much and I'm so sorry for what my dad has done to you."

I went upstairs and washed my face. I looked in the mirror and my eyes were all puffed up. I was to go and meet Silvia in Bolton to sort out my passport and to book my holiday for Amsterdam.

I walked up the road totally oblivious of what was going around me. Birth certificate in hand I started to dwell upon my youth. Everybody knew me as Minihane. It was time to bury the past once and for all. I was called Lomax now and as from today that would be my name. I caught the red bus to Bolton and met Silvia outside the post office on Churchgate. She looked stunning as usual in her tight jeans and white blouse. The form for the passport had already been signed by my parents. The guy behind the counter had a quick look and replied everything was in order. It brought a huge smile of relief and to my face and I gave Silvia a big kiss on the lips to show my appreciation. It was time to go and book our holiday to Amsterdam

We called at the travel shop and found a three-day trip to Amsterdam, it was as cheap as chips. Traveling down by coach to Hull and a short mini cruise to Rotterdam and then by coach to Amsterdam, we would be spending two nights on board but with enough time to explore Amsterdam to see the sites.

It would be six weeks later when we would both travel to Amsterdam and three weeks before that when I received my passport.

The day had arrived. I got up early, which was unusual for me. I had already done the packing the night before. As usual, my mum was already up cooking my breakfast. Boiled egg and soldiers (toast) and a hot cup of tea with two digestive biscuits.

She sat down at the table and then held my hand and said, "I hope you have a great time with Silvia. I have made you a few sandwiches and given you some pop and crisps."

I replied, "Thanks mum, I really appreciate it."

She always finished off by saying, "be careful Ian."

I said my goodbyes and kissed my mum on the cheek giving her a cuddle and I was on my way, small black suitcase in hand.

I headed up Derwent Road to catch the bus to Bolton as I was meeting Silvia at Moor Lane bus station. It was from there that we were being picked up.

I was looking forward to the trip. Amsterdam with its canals, clogs, cheese, flowers, cafes and friendly faces. The Netherlands was one of Europe's warmest welcomes.

It's always been an open-minded, tolerant country, reflected in the accepting, laid-back nature of the Dutch people.

Silvia was already there waiting for the coach. She looked radiant with her sparking blue eyes. At the side of her was her suitcase or should I say 'kitchen sink'. She brought enough clothes with her to last a month. The coach pulled in and I could feel the excitement. The driver struggled to lift Silvia's case so I had to give him a lift. The coach set off on time and we stopped at different bus stops, picking up other people on the way. As we sat on the coach Silvia cuddled me and we had the odd kiss which seemed to annoy a few passengers in front but it was a good trip down and we stopped for a breather a few times at the motorway services. We finally arrived at the port in Hull.

Hull's (its full title is Kingston-Upon-Hull) maritime pre-eminence dates back to 1299, when it was laid out as a seaport by Edward I. It quickly became England's leading harbour, and was still a vital garrison when the gates were closed against Charles I in 1642. This was the first serious act of rebellion of what was to become the English Civil War. The port of Hull is on the north bank of the Humber Estuary and is just 20 miles from the North Sea. It was now early in the evening and the ferry to Rotterdam was a night sailing so we had a couple of hours to chill out. We had a couple of coffees and a little walk round and before we knew it was time to get back on the coach as it was time to embark onto the ferry. It was a slow process with the large number of coaches and cars and then having our passports collected and checked.

After all the kerfuffle, we were shown to our cabins. It was quite spacious with a small wash basin and two bunk beds; quite comfortable. We quickly washed ourselves down, changed and headed for the top deck. We held each other as we watched the ship leave Hull harbour. My mind drifted back to the time I sailed across the English Channel. I was just fourteen years old and missing my mother. It was different this time. I was happy and actually looking forward to our destination. We had a few drinks in one of the bars. I had a couple of beers and Silvia had a couple of rum and blacks (black currant juice) with ice. We decided to head for our cabin as we were tired after the long trip down to Hull and to be truthful, I was grateful as I could feel my stomach going a little and I felt slightly sick. My legs were a bit wobbly. I felt as if I was drunk after a drinking session on a night out around Bolton. It was sea sickness of course and it was time to make a swift exit to the toilets. I just made it as I vomited in the toilet. I felt rough. I looked in the mirror and my face looked green.

I was in the toilet a good twenty minutes when I could hear Silvia shouting, outside the toilet door, "You ok Ian?"

I wasn't but I put a brave face on as I came out the toilet. The crossing wasn't that rough but it affected me. I headed straight for my bunk bed. I slept on the bottom one so it was easier for me to get to the sink if I felt sick. I slept like a log for which I was very grateful as I felt so ill. Hull to Rotterdam was roughly 240 miles and took about 11 hours, if I remember.

Then it was time to find our way to the coach as we had finally arrived at the docks of Rotterdam. We went through all the kerfuffle again having the passports checked but it soon passed. I was very excited as Silvia soon found out with the number of times I squeezed her and kissed her lips. Rotterdam was about 55 miles to Amsterdam so it didn't take long. I looked at the scenery and I was fascinated by the land which seemed to be very flat and there were plenty of green areas with the odd sprinkle of windmills and villages along the way.

We finally arrived in Amsterdam. It didn't take long, just a few hours. We parked up not far from the city centre. As we got off the coach we were all handed a map (guide of Amsterdam.) The driver told us we had to be back at the coach for 6pm. That gave us a good day to explore the sights.

Amsterdam was a very attractive place, a 17th century historical atmosphere combined with the mentality of a modern metropolis which created a friendly and relaxed environment. The small scale of the buildings and the intimacy of the narrow streets, canals and squares, visitors find unique. The city has the highest museum density in the world. It also had famous enough residents including Ann Frank the diarist and the artist Rembrandt, van Rijn and Vincent van Goth to name a few. We headed for Dam square which was packed with food stalls cafes and restaurants and shops galore. The square was packed with tourists. There was some entertainment, like a clown entertaining the kids with his tricks. There were plenty of buskers and even live statutes who would tap you on the shoulder if you walked past them without dropping a few coins into his little bowl. There we saw odd group of hippies smoking and it was obvious, it was cannabis.

The bars and cafes were packed. Most people spoke English which helped. We took plenty of pictures and some outside the Royal Palace. (Koninklijk Palace.) This was where the royal family lived.

The pigeons were in abundance and sometimes you had to duck as they dive-bombed over your heads for the odd scraps of food that the tourist used to leave on the ground. I was in total awe of the place.

Silvia was getting hungry so we headed for a cafe to sample the local cuisine. I had the Dutch version of French Fries, 'Friet'. They are thicker than the normal French Fries and invented in the northern part of Belgium. The Dutch really like them especially with a lot of toppings such as mayonnaise, tomato ketchup, curry or peanut sauce. A famous combination of toppings is mayonnaise, raw chopped onions and peanut sauce and is called a 'patatje oorlog' (fries at war). It is tasty, but it does not look that way. I also had 'Bitterballen' a savoury meat ball which was fried in deep oil. Silvia had 'Erwtensoep' or 'Snert' is made of split peas, celery, leeks, carrots and pork. This pea soup is a very thick soup. The thick 'Erwtensoep' is traditionally eaten during the winter with slices of 'rookworst' (smoked sausage) and rye bread with 'katenspek' (a type of Dutch bacon, first cooked and then smoked). We also had a couple of beers to swill it down as we watched all the tourists passing us by on the square.

We headed for the canals which ran through the city centre and as we walked hand in hand we saw hundreds of people on bikes pedalling along the labyrinth streets. We walked along the canals which were packed with markets and cafes. The canal boats were beautiful and in the windows, you could see sprinkles of red flowers. There were also plenty of tourists on the barges taking in the famous sights of Amsterdam, along the way. It was very romantic. Silvia and I held hands and had plenty of cuddles along the way. Silvia asked me if I wanted to go into one of the cannabis cafes for a laugh. I replied, "No thanks. I don't do drugs," much to her annoyance.

We decided to go to the famous Red Light district which was famous all over the world. From brothels to sex shops, to museums, the Amsterdam Red Light district leaves nothing to the imagination. It is very likely that you will have heard about this neighbourhood and to be frank, everything you will have heard is probably true, but to really put rumours to rest, you need to check it out for yourself. The *Rossebuurt,* as the locals know it, is unlike any other place. Guaranteed.

Certainly, the Red-Light district in Amsterdam, that everyone knows about is the one where women, of all nationalities, parade their wares in red-fringed window parlours, many ready to offer more than a school boy peep-show in a private cabin.

Another familiar sight in the Amsterdam Red Light district is of packs of men, young and old, couples holding hands and pointing in shock at it all, giggling groups of women celebrating hen nights and busloads of Japanese tourists toting cameras (except not in the direction of the female entertainers! Strictly banned!)

Silvia wanted to buy a souvenir from one of the sex shops. I went red in the face as I had never been in one She bought herself a blue vibrator It was the first time I had ever seen one. I decided to wait outside the shop as I was embarrassed.

The day passed very quickly and it was time to head back to our coach. We were late leaving Amsterdam as one of the elderly couples had a heart attack and was taken to the local hospital. We slept most of the journey back as we were tired after all the walking and the excitement of seeing Amsterdam.

Not long after that, Silvia and I split up. She found company with a lad from Blackburn who she met through her parents. Another reason why I hated anybody associated with the name Blackburn. I was upset for a while but I soon got over her. As the old saying goes, *there are plenty more fish in the sea*. As for the trip to Amsterdam it was a fantastic experience and memorable one.

Chapter Thirty-Nine

Blackpool Riviera

Blackpool was well known for its hen and stag parties and pub crawls and the odd knee trembler in the long winding back streets. I wanted to taste a sample of all that. I already visited Blackpool once when I was young kid when I ran in to the sea fully clothed. And in 1974 when I went watching Bolton Wanderers against Blackpool when a young Blackpool fan, Kevin Olsen tragically lost his life. He was murdered on the old Kop terracing at Bloomfield Road.

On Mick's birthday, we decided, with a few other close friends, that we would spend the weekend in Blackpool for a good piss up and hopefully a few encounters with the girls. He would be seventeen years old, the same age as I was and the others. We were all working and on good money so it was easily affordable.

Frank sorted everything out; the hotel and the date. I remember the day well, it was a hot summer's day in July, a Saturday and the day I had been looking forward to.

I walked up Derwent Road with my small hold-all (bag) with all the necessities I needed for the trip. I even brought some Brut after-shave so I would smell nice for the girls. I didn't realise at the time that every other young, hot-blooded male was wearing it at the time. The bars and clubs smelt like a perfume factory, such was the strong scent.

There would be five of us going on the trip. Frank, Alan. Mick and a friend of Frank's (his name was Dave but everybody called him Hercules. He was huge and built like a brick shit house with muscles to burn and the looks to go with it and sure to be a hit with the girls) and then there was me. We all met up at Bolton train station and we caught the

10.30 train to Blackpool. The trip took about an hour and on the way, all we talked about was beer and girls. Frank pulled a bottle of vodka out of a plastic bag and by the end of the trip we had drunk the whole bottle. I was already feeling a bit tipsy and a bit nauseous and I had to make a few trips to the toilet where I vomited profusely and blocked the toilet. I even filled the washing basin. The toilet stank of sick and not many people used the toilet on the way to Blackpool.

We finally arrived at Blackpool north and I felt a little better after the vomiting. We headed straight to the Bed and breakfast (hotel). We seemed to be walking for ages along the pier and back streets It must have been a good thirty minutes.

I was constantly whingeing at Frank and he turned around to me, "Ian, we are here. There it is, the white building on the corner?"

We booked ourselves in at the reception with a woman who was in her late 40s. She was huge and the ugliest woman I have ever seen in my life. She had no teeth in and I couldn't understand a word she said. She wasn't someone you would like to meet in some dark alley. She gave me the creeps.

I bunked in with Frank and the other three slept in a double room with two single beds and a sofa-bed. The hotel didn't look nice. The wall paper was hanging off the walls. Most of the light switches weren't working and a couple of them had electrical wires hanging down. Our room was no better. I turned the light on and the bulb exploded which frightened the life out of me. We had two single beds which each had a sheet and one blanket. This brought back memories of Lee Street in the early impoverished times. We had an electric fire but it had no plug on it. The curtains rails were hanging off and we couldn't open the windows as they were nailed into the woodwork. To make matters worse,

Frank turned a picture round and it fell off the wall. I felt more at home in some of the cells I had visited in my youth in Farnworth. Enough of the whingeing, we unpacked and called on the others and they were also whingeing at the condition of the rooms. We decided to go for a meal and we had fish, chips and mushy peas.

We had a walk around the pier for a while and then we headed to the famous Blackpool Pleasure Beach. We had a couple of rides on the Grand National and the Mad Mouse and then we decided to go for a drink in the Manchester which was a pub I frequented before, when Bolton Wanderers played Blackpool in 1974. It was one of their main pubs in Blackpool at the time and if I remember, Bolton fans smashed all the windows after the Blackpool fans refused to come out.

There were a couple of bouncers outside the doors so I told Frank to let Dave go in first as he looked a lot older then us but he was told, under no circumstances, must we mention we were from Bolton because of the Blackpool fan that died and the locals still felt a lot of resentment towards the Bolton people. We were all let in but only after one of the tattooed bouncers gave me the once over. The pub was packed to the rafters you could hardly move. We got talking to a few girls from Wigan and we arranged to meet them later in the night.

I had a few kisses with one of them. I can't remember her name now but she caught my attention straight away. You guessed it, she had massive boobs which was the first thing I always looked for, in a girl. We had a couple of cuddles as you do and I made sure I had a good feel of her boobs near the toilets and I was told that was all I was getting till later

I came out of the toilet and I saw Frank and Alan chatting to a few lads who were sitting in the corner. I looked around to see where Dave and Mick were and then, in the corner of my eye, I saw them both coming out of the toilets with two girls in tandem. Dave had a huge grin on his face and he winked at me to say he got what he wanted. I was just going to say something to Dave when I heard a table get turned over and a few glasses getting smashed. Frank had hit one of the lads he was chatting to earlier. When all hell broke loose, there were five of us against three of them so it was no match for us. I hit one and knocked him over the table and Dave who was built like a brick shit house destroyed two of them who ran for their lives and headed for the exit doors. Within minutes, three of the bouncers dragged Frank, Alan and me out. Dave just casually walked out with Alan in tow, without the bouncers saying a single word to them which didn't surprise me in view of the size of Dave.

We decided to head back to the hotel and along the way I asked Frank what started it all and he just laughed and said, "One of them called me a Bolton bastard so I hit him and then all hell broke loose."

I replied, "I told you not to mention where we were from."

He shrugged his shoulders and said he couldn't help it after they told him they were Blackpool fans. It was like a red rag to a bull.

We changed and I put my brut on to make sure I smelled nice. Then we all headed to a cafe on the front for something to eat. We all had something simple. The majority had meat pies with mashed potatoes and veg followed by ice cream.

We couldn't go back in the Manchester as we were all barred after the earlier fracas with the Blackpool lads so we decided to give that a wide berth. I just wanted to have fun with the girls, that's all I came for.

We all headed for the bars on the front. They were all full with lads in fancy dress, from Robin Hood to Batman. The girls were mostly in dresses or tight jeans with tight low tops some of which caught my eye straight away, with their large breasts and the high wedged shoes they were wearing.

The night was going well. We mixed in with crowds and got chatting with the girls who came from all over the country just as the lads did. They came from as far as Glasgow, Aberdeen and London.

About 11 pm we decided to head for the 007 night-club. The 007 in Blackpool began life as an upmarket nightclub. It's proprietor, heavy weight boxer Brian London, was a draw in himself, but with his sporting buddies frequenting the venue it did no harm to the reputation of the club.

From its genesis in the early 1970s it attracted locals and visitors alike who were more than happy to don suits and frocks befitting the themed décor and style. On the ground-floor, comfortable booths surrounded a dance floor set out to resemble the ring of the boxing arena with ropes as partitions. Portraits of the boxing world's elite festooned the walls.

Up here was more genteel, the music more for couples to sashay around the floor. Downstairs was darker, louder, and a more frenetic side of the nightclub scene of the early 70s, with foot-tapping chart tunes from Glam Rock to Soul, where the more danceable side of the 60s also prevailed.

However, by the mid/late 70s, and the continuing UK economic downturn the numbers began to drop as money became tighter and the party atmosphere receded, not only for the club, but for the town as a whole.

1976 saw numbers that broke recent records as the heatwave brought visitors to the beach in droves. 1977

(Jubilee year) marked the beginning of a recession for the town that it is still recovering from in many ways.

As for The 007, it was a venue in need of a beating heart... And God created Punk.

As the coiffured ladies and suits grew fewer in the queue for the 007 on Topping Street, the leather jacketed Mohawks and Doc-donned Skins increased. This new clientèle commandeered the basement dance-floor while, in some cases, their parents (generation) continued to enjoy the upstairs.

This was the birth of what was to become the 'Legendary' 007 club in Blackpool, that would endure for almost half a decade before it's premature demise.

There were large queues outside and they were literally lined up in hundreds, three deep. The bouncers were like beer monsters. They were huge. They even put Dave in the shade, such was the size of them. Many people got turned away for being drunk and that included the girls. There was the odd scuffle in the queues as the frustration boiled over with the time it was taking to get in. Everybody was searched for weapons and for trying to smuggle drink in. It took nearly two hours to get in.

We headed for the dance floor and it was packed with girls which made us happy, as the competition was on to see who kissed the most girls. I decided I was going to enjoy the night and not to get too drunk as I wanted to have fun.

At the bar, we saw the girls we met earlier. It didn't take Dave long. He was straight in with his usual chat-up lines which more than often worked for him. He pulled all the girls with his good looks and his muscular body which attracted all the girls. I got talking to the blonde piece I chatted to earlier with the huge breasts which seemed to pop out of her low white top. I found out her name. She was called Pam. She was 18 years old and was a student nurse from Wigan. We danced most of the night and smooched to the odd Diana Ross tune. And now and again my hand would feel her breast under her white top which she didn't seem to mind after a few drinks.

The night was interrupted by a few minor scuffles but the bouncers soon put a stop to that by giving them a few slaps and dragging them out of the nightclub. At the end of the night we all decided to leave with the girls in tow. Every one of us had copped off. We all decided to go for a walk on the beach and we all separated to do what was necessary or get our wicked way, so to speak. I just grabbed Pam and started kissing her with my tongue. I was like an octopus my hands were everywhere. I pushed her down on the sand and started to caress her breast which seemed to excite her. I then slowly unzipped her pants and push them down and she did the same to me it wasn't long before my penis was standing to attention. Pam put her hand down on to my crotch and started to pleasure me. I couldn't take any more. I pulled her white knickers down and I climbed on top of her and we started to have sex. It lasted for a good ten minutes then she climbed on top of me and she was like a steam train. I couldn't keep up with her she was going crazy with excitement. She bit my neck and left a few marks and she bit my lips. I felt as though I had been ten rounds with a heavy-weight boxer. My back was scratched, my lip was swollen and I had marks on my neck but it was well worth it. Another notch on my bed post. After it was all over we chatted for a bit and then we walked back casually and met the others.

Frank was still at it with the blonde bimbo and they made more noise than they did at Burnden Park, the home of Bolton Wanderers.

Mick was slowly getting dressed as was Alan but David was dressed and just chatting to a bird with long red hair. We decided to walk them all home as they invited us all back for a drink which didn't take much persuasion.

We were walking down the back street when we saw about 20 lads and as they got closer it was the Blackpool lads we fought with earlier. I turned around to Frank and I told them we must do a runner and meet up with the girls later. But David wanted to fight them all on his own. He was as mad as a hatter. As they got closer and closer we noticed some of them had knifes. It was time to disappear. We all ran and left the girls to it. Frank and I ran off together and the others went their separate ways. I was tripped up from behind and they were all over me like a shot. There was nothing I could do. I was kicked all over the floor.

I was lying in a pool of blood and all I remember was Frank picking me up and telling me I had been hit over the head with a bottle. My legs felt like jelly. I was covered in blood. My head and my back were killing me. I knew I had had a good kicking. Frank told me I need to go to the hospital for stitches as my head was split open.

Within minutes the cavalry turned up. I looked at Dave, his black shirt was ripped apart, his left eye was swelling and obviously going black. He showed me his hands which were like shovels. They were covered in blood.

He was laughing. He said, with a huge grin, "I leathered two of them and beat them badly. They scarpered when they saw their mates got a good hammering."

This brought a smile to my face. All of us, had some kind of injuries.

Frank was typical he just blurted out, "We will do them again when Bolton play them."

We all just burst out laughing. I already decided I wasn't going to the hospital till I got home. We all went back to the bed and breakfast and we all chatted till the early hours laughing and boasting about our conquests with the girls.

The following day we had a few beers in a bar near the station then it was time for home. My head was still banging and pouring with blood. I called at the hospital before I went home so as not to worry my mum. I had four stitches in my head wound and it would be a good few days before my head would stop hurting.

Blackpool was a good experience and I enjoyed our first week-end away. As for the fighting, I just took it as a normal night out in Farnworth where fighting on a Saturday night was the norm.

Chapter Forty

The French Foreign Legion

At the age of eighteen I decided to leave home once again and this time I was more determined to leave for good. Even though the abuse had stopped with my father the pain and the anger I felt towards him had never left me. I had made my mind up that I had to cut loose from my mother's apron strings; it was time to find my own way in the world. My mother always knew that I would leave one day to seek for my own way in life.

The day had arrived, my suitcase was packed. I knew where I was staying as I had already done my homework. I wanted to live outside Bolton away from my family and friends.

I wanted to start afresh in a new place and to make new friends. I hugged my mother and told her how much I loved her. As usual she stayed calm and tried not to show her feelings.

Before I left she held my hand and then put something in my pocket. Then she said to me, "Ian keep out of trouble and look after yourself."

I just smiled and then I left. I never said goodbye to my father as he kept well out of my way. My dad showed no compassion or any interest and our feelings towards each other were mutual. As I was walking up the path I put my hand in my pocket and felt some paper. I looked and it was thirty pounds in an elastic band. I looked up and my mother was smiling and waving at me through the window.

I waved and smiled back and then I turned away and carried on walking. I never turned back as I was frightened I would change my mind and go back home.

I made my way to the bus stop at the top of my road and while I was waiting, I was reminiscing about my younger days, the troubles I used to get up to. I could see the police houses where Sergeant Swann used to live and the shops where I used to hang around with my friends. It was here that I had had to grow up very quickly and learn how to defend myself. The petty thieving, the gang fights and the run-ins with the infamous Sergeant Swann; it was now time to put it all behind me and move on to pastures new.

The bus arrived and I jumped on and sat down. I looked through the window as the bus was leaving. I had a big smile on my face. I thought to myself I had some great memories but my troubles were over. It was a new beginning now or so I thought.

I stayed in a bed-and-breakfast in Swinton. It was cheap and just a few miles from Farnworth and it was easy access to get to and from work.

Swinton is a town within the City of Salford, in Greater Manchester. (Historically in Lancashire)

I arrived in the afternoon at the B & B and I was met by the owner at the door. He introduced himself and took me to my room.

The room was not big; in fact, it was quite small with a bed and a small bed-side cabinet. There was a wardrobe and that was it. The carpets were brown and worn and the curtains were a dirty cream colour and they weren't hanging correctly as the curtain rail was hanging off the wall.

The owner then showed me the bathroom which had to be shared with the other guests. It was smaller than my old box-room at home.

It was certainly a wake-up call and reality started to sink in. I soon realised that there was no place like home.

I unpacked what clothes I had and I decided to have a few hours' nap. I found it difficult to sleep, however, as my thoughts kept drifting back to my youth and my bond with my mother.

I was soon settled and the trips to work every day took my mind off other things. One night I was sitting alone in a pub near to where I was staying. Little did I expect a chance encounter with a stranger that would lead me to another journey and one that would leave me scared for the rest of my life?

It all started with, "Hi mate, do you mind if I join you?" He introduced himself and said his name was Paul Smith. The conversation soon got on to football which was a favourite passion in life for us both. He was a Manchester

United supporter and with me being a Bolton Wanderers supporter it didn't go down too well with me. However, with me being alone, I carried on with the conversation.

Paul smith was nothing special to look at. He was tall and skinny with long scruffy brown hair.

He stuttered quite badly which seemed to improve the more he drank and throughout the evening I got to learn his life-story.

He had been in and out of Borstal (A Borstal was the term used to describe a system of juvenile detention centres that existed in the United Kingdom for most of the 20th century) and in and out of adult prisons.

The conversation soon got around to the French foreign Legion as he started to open up about his life of crime.

He then told me he was on the run from the police and if they caught him, he was going to get sent down again.

That's when he turned around and told me he wanted to join the French legion in a bid to be a better person, as they give you a new identity; a new name, passport and a new life and a new family. The French Foreign Legion would look after you with a pension and a new life.

I laughed out loud and told him he had watched too many films. I watched Beau Geste and I didn't fancy having my head stuck in the sand, to which he replied with a smile, "It's not like that Ian, I have looked into it."

That's when I realised he was serious and I started to wonder, would it erase my past of beatings at the hands of my father?

Paul then came straight out with it. "Why don't you come too?" Suddenly, it just seemed exciting, a new adventure.

I said "Yes" and we arranged to meet the following day. That's when I found out he had nowhere to stay. He had told me he was on the run from the police so I decided to smuggle Paul into the B & B.

We both talked quietly through the night. We were like two excited kids.

I asked Paul what age you had to be to join the legion.

He then replied, "18."

I then asked, "Where do you join-up for the legion?"

Paul responded "Paris".

I didn't know whether to laugh or cry and told Paul I ran away to Paris when I was fourteen.

We both just laughed and Paul said, "This time it will be better."

In the morning, I went down for a full English breakfast (egg, bacon, tomatoes, fried bread with toast and a mug of coffee.) I smuggled a few bacon sandwiches out for Paul.

I packed a few essentials for my journey whereas Paul just had the clothes he was wearing along with his passport and about forty pounds which was from a cheque he had stolen.

I telephoned my boss at the place where I worked and told him I was sick and I didn't know when I would be coming back. Then we made our way to the post office where I paid for a temporary short-term passport and then we were off.

We caught a train from Piccadilly train-station to London. The journey down was uneventful and we then caught a train to Dover.

We weren't hanging around for long before we were on the ferry to Calais. As the ship sailed away I could see the white cliffs of Dover and for a spit second it brought back the memories and feelings of my first trip to Paris

The trip was still uneventful and the conversation between us was short as we only talked about football. I wonder now if it could have been our misapprehension and fear of the unknown preventing us from talking about what lay ahead.

After a couple of hours, we arrived at Calais and we made our way to the bottom deck and ready to disembark.

We both just followed the queues until we had our passports checked and then we made our way to the train station.

When we arrived at the train station there were thousands of tourists of different nationalities from different parts of Europe. It didn't take us long to find the ticket-office. We then booked our relevant tickets to continue our journey to Paris.

The journey took just under four hours and soon passed. Paul had suddenly regained his enthusiasm. The conversation was non-stop about the French Foreign Legion and he was so excited about the prospect of being a soldier in the famous army.

On the other hand, I was slightly nervous and wary of what I was getting myself into. Before we knew it, we had arrived in Paris.

We made our way out of the train-station and headed for the centre of Paris. I was so excited. I kept telling Paul that Paris was the most interesting city in Europe and probably one of the most amazing cities worldwide. People from all over the world, travel to Paris. They come to discover and experience this fairy-tale city. Paris was the city of love, inspiration, art and fashion. The night-scene, the Eiffel tower, I continued until he abruptly ended my conversation and told me we are not here to be a tourist but to enlist in the French Foreign Legion.

He then told me we must ask someone how to get to the Fort de Nogent as time was getting on.

We approached a French policeman. They are known as Gendarmes. We asked him how to get to the Fort de Nogent? He smiled and said, "The foreign legion?" He then said, "Follow me," in good English. "I will show you the bus to get you there."

He showed us the bus-stop where we were to catch the bus and then he laughed and walked off to our amusement.

We didn't wait too long as buses were quite frequent. We jumped on the bus and said to the driver, "Fort de Nogent?" He just replied, "Three francs."

We both paid the amount and sat down. The journey wasn't long but it was a very interesting trip. Nevertheless, I showed Paul the Eifel Tower and some of the places where I begged and tried to pick pockets.

The journey was short and the bus stopped and the driver shouted, "Fort de Nogent," so we got off and in the distance, we could see a large building with an imposing arch and gates.

I said to Paul, "We are here. Are you sure you don't want to change your mind?"

He smiled and said, "Come on Ian, we have a new life now, a new future."

We reached the Fort and there was a traffic circle with a huge sign indicating *Legion Etrangere* off to the side.

There was what appeared to be a tree-lined driveway next to the sign that led down between two apartment buildings. We both walked to the sign. We walked down the driveway and eventually the stone walls and gate of a very ancient looking fortress came into view. There was no doubt in my mind that this was the place as above the gate were the words *Legion Etrangere*. At this point, I got a tingling sensation down my neck. The most complicated part of our trip was now over.

We walked through the gates and we were approached by what we took to be a legionnaire dressed in a blue boiler suit. Paul spoke and said we wished to join the legion.

The legionnaire gestured to us to follow him. He took us to a reception area where were met by another legionnaire who was sitting behind a desk.

We were then taken separately into different rooms. It was there that we handed over our passports. The legionnaire then asked me various questions about my age and country of origin. He then enquired if we had any criminal records. Were we wanted by the police? It was then that I started to worry about Paul; if he would tell the truth or would he lie.

I filled all the paperwork in and he explained all about the legion, the length of service and the army pensions etc.

I was then told I would have to have a medical before I was accepted into the legion. Then he said that I should go into another room and to get undressed as I was having a medical there and then.

I didn't wait long until one of the army doctors came in. He asked a lot of questions about my health and then I was subject to a thorough examination.

I was then told to get dressed and wait. After a few minutes, I was escorted to another room where Paul was already there with a few other recruits.

It was here that I was told that I had to fill in the relevant forms before I could be accepted into the legion.

We were only at the centre for a few days and when it came time for us to leave the Fort (when there were enough of us and we had been through our preliminary medical examinations) we showered and dressed in our civilian clothes. We were then placed on a bus and taken to a large train station in Paris (I think it was Gare de Lyon.)

We rode on an overnight train to Marseille that stopped many times along the way. We had our own seats, but had to share the car with tourists and local commuters.

We were accompanied by three legionnaires but they were dressed in civvies. We were told by one of the legionnaires, a corporal I think, that we needed permission to go to the toilet or the bathroom so that they knew where we were.

The train journey was bad because I couldn't get any sleep. You could hear people walking up and down the train and some of the passengers even brought their dogs and you could hear them barking now and again. The most annoying was the conductor he would turn the lights on checking the passengers' tickets.

When we arrived in Marseille, the sun was already up. We exited the train and made our way to another platform where we boarded a double-decker local commuter train to Aubagne. When we arrived in Aubagne, a bus was waiting to take us to Quartier Vienot, the HQ of the Legion.

The first thing we did at Aubagne was to get our pictures taken. They resembled prisoner mug-shots. Afterwards, we were marched a short way to a small white building which would be our home until either going to basic training or being dismissed. We walked around to a side door to the basement where we met a Corporal who would be with us the whole time we were there. We then had to strip down (including our underwear) to be naked. They issued us underwear, shorts, a T-shirt, socks and a really crappy pair of flat-soled zero-support zero-cushioning tennis shoes. Our names were then called one by one and we went up to a counter with our bag, (filled with the clothes we had just gotten out of.) There a legionnaire took inventory of what we had. I had to sign the inventory and then grab the military backpack and run around to the other side of the counter and sit down and wait with guys who had gone before me. The Corporal explained the rules to us (in French) with accompanying gesturing for emphasis. He was the boss. He's the Legionnaire. We want to be like him. We don't talk. We do what he says. The only place where you can talk and do what you want is in the back of the building. There, he said, we could talk, smoke, snort our cocaine if we wanted. He strongly recommended, however, that we spend our time running and doing push-ups. He said that in basic training there will be many push-ups. We were later shown to our room where we were assigned our bunks.

We woke up at somewhere around 3:30 - 4:00 am every day and were supposed to go to sleep at around 9:00 pm (you usually could not go to sleep until a couple of hours after 9:00 because most people in your room would keep talking.) We took showers before going to bed, and it was the same deal as in Paris - not enough time and a whole lot of guys scrambling for a few showers. The guys who got to the showers first tended to take their sweet time and the guys stuck at the end would have to rush. We had to clean our room every day and fold our sheets a certain way immediately after waking up, and make the bed a certain way immediately before going to bed. When not on a work detail or taking a test, we sat in a large 'garden' behind the building that was devoid of grass. There, people tended to group together by language/ethnic background and talk with each other. There were probably over a couple of hundred guys there all the time. People seemed to disappear every day and new faces appeared to replace them. Some people exercised, but most just sat around smoking and talking.

I received my first haircut and to my horror they shaved off all my hair. I felt so naked. I was then kitted out with my new army uniform. My best friend was my new beret to cover the modesty of my bald head.

When I saw Paul I just burst out laughing his head was shaven like mine but he looked like a matchstick as he was so thin.

Life was pretty boring in the legion at the beginning. There was a klaxon (air raid siren) mounted on the roof of the building at the rear. When it went off, all the CEVs in the 'garden' would take off running -- just like a stampede -- towards the front of the building where there was a large tarmac that served as a formation area. We would have to quickly get into a block formation and stand at attention (known as 'gardez-vous.') When in block formation we would be split up to handle work details, or take tests, or go eat a meal, or be yelled at for something, or made to do push-ups, sit-ups, roll-over, or other punitive exercises. Many times, we would get called to the formation, then have to walk around the building en masse and pick up 'debris' (cigarette butts, trash, sometimes rocks, leaves, etc...). Sometimes we would have to go, 'weed the canal' next to the building. Mainly, picking up debris and weeding the canal were just busy work for us. Work details included cleaning our barracks, doing kitchen duty in one of several kitchens: either the main kitchen, a satellite kitchen elsewhere in the base, at Malmousque -- the Legion resort, or at the Legion retirement home. There were also non-kitchen work details at these locations as well as 'debris' collection elsewhere in the base. I wound up doing kitchen duty in the main kitchen a lot, mainly because I happened to be around after a meal when the mess hall (salles de manger) Corporal was looking for people to do kitchen duty. I really didn't mind because I found that, generally, the Legionnaires that worked in the kitchens were really cool guys who were [usually] pretty laid back. A major problem that develops at Aubagne is dehydration. It is very hard to stay adequately hydrated because you always have to drink from a tap and access to the interior of the building is restricted (even to go to the toilet.)

Paul and I became quite friendly with two lads; a lad from Dublin who we called paddy and a lad from Holland who we called Dutch for obvious reasons.

We would spend many an hour chatting about our experiences in our own countries and the reasons why we joined the legion.

Paddy pre-warned me about some of the cliques in the legion and I was told in no uncertain terms to keep my nose clean and not to get involved with anybody else's squabbles. He had seen a few legionnaires get a good hiding and it was taboo to tell tales to any senior officers. It would be a death sentence to anybody who grassed anyone up.

I looked at Paul with a worried look but he just burst out laughing and said stop worrying, "We are all family in here."

What happened next would turn my career in the legion upside down and become a nightmare which would haunt me for the rest of my life. It all started when I walked into the shower room with Paul and I saw three males of Arab descent beating up a male who was known to be a Jew. I intervened by grabbing one of the Arabs who I threw against the shower wall. I then punched one of the other Arabs who let go of the Jewish lad. The Jewish male then grabbed his towel and ran out. The attention turned to me. I was pushed against the wall and I was being punched and kicked at will.

It was over before it started as more legionnaires came in to the showers. Before the Arabs left I was warned in broken English that my life was in danger and to watch my back.

I went crazy at Paul and I shouted why didn't he help me? His pitiful reply was that I was told to keep my nose clean and not to get involved. I grabbed Paul by the neck and called him a fucking coward and as I walked away he shouted to me not go to the officers and tell them what happened, as it would be a death sentence for me and it would not be safe for me to stay in the legion. I just looked at him in disgust. I got dressed and walked away.

I was only in the legion a couple of weeks and I was already regretting every minute.

I was still having medicals and doing physical tests and interviews and this carried on for days. I was doing plenty of running and sit-ups under the watchful eyes of the trainers. I heard if you failed the test you would be kicked out the same day.

I still had a few friends in the legion. Paddy and Dutch were always by my side and as for Paul he went into a shell. He wasn't the same person any more. He tried to avoid me when he could and we only ever spoke a few words.

Things turned from bad to worse in the early hours of the morning when I was asleep. I felt a hand running up and down my body. It woke me up. Besides my bed were two of the Arabs who attacked me in the shower. One of them put his hands over my mouth while the other one was trying to hold me down on the bed and tried to grab my penis.

I was kicking out like crazy. I was biting the Arab's hand as hard as I could.

Dutch jumped out of his bunk and ran to my aid.

The two Arabs ran off to their bunks. I was shaking with fear. My emotions were all over the place. I was disgusted I wanted to go to the shower and wash myself clean but I was too afraid to go in case they followed me in there.

Dutch sat on my bed for a few hours trying to calm me down. He kept telling I must not report it as things would look bad for me.

I didn't sleep all night and I was more determined now to watch my back and keep out of trouble.

I always made sure I was with Dutch and Paddy whenever I went for a shower and that I was never on my own.

My moods and my desire to be in the legion had changed. I had only been in the legion a few weeks but it was becoming a life sentence of fear and intimidation.

I was still getting the occasional punch and kick on the legs from the Arabs whenever it suited them to do so.

I couldn't retaliate as I would have been in serious trouble. I couldn't do a runner as I would have been charged with desertion.

Things came to ahead when I was having my breakfast and one of the Arabs threw a tray over me and spat in my face.

I wanted to kill him on the spot but Dutch held me down. The Arab walked away, laughing.

I told Dutch I was brought up with violence and been involved in gangs and football violence but this was on a different scale.

I have never been so afraid. I told Dutch I had only been in the legion a few weeks but I had to get out before I did something stupid.

Dutch replied, "Follow me. I will tell you how to get out of the legion."

I walked past the smirking Arabs and just smiled at them and gave them the 'wankers' sign. I passed Paul and he put his head down and ignored me. I shouted to him that he was also a 'wanker' and I walked out of the dining room.

Dutch and Paddy were waiting for me. I followed them into the toilets so we could speak in private.

I asked Dutch to tell me how could get out of the legion. He replied the only way was to harm myself. You will be kicked out of the legion for cowardice; a dishonourable discharge.

I shook both their hands and thanked them. I went to my locker and got hold off a razor blade. Then I cut a little on my wrist, enough to make it bleed. I let the blood run down my arm and on to my green uniform to make it look worse. Then I told Dutch to go and tell the Corporal. Within minutes the Corporal came running in. He slapped my face and called me a coward and told me to go and clean myself up then to report to his office straight away.

I looked at Dutch and Paddy and smiled and winked. Then I went to the toilet and cleaned myself up.

I knocked on the door of the Corporal's office and he shouted in his French accent, "Come in Mr Lomax." I went in and the Corporal was with an officer. I was then told to shut the door and sit down.

On the table were some documents. I was told I was being discharged from the legion and that I would not be allowed to return.

I signed my signature and then I was frog-marched into a small room. Inside I found my small suitcase containing the clothes I came in. I was told to sign another document for the items I received.

The corporal told me to strip off my uniform. While I was doing this, he stood and watched.

He then kicked my army kit to one side and shouted to me to get dressed. He said the sooner I was off this camp the better.

I knew he was trying to humiliate me but I didn't care. I was going home. As soon as I was dressed he shouted, "Follow me, English coward."

I was taken to a counter where my passport was handed to me and a small packet with a few hundred francs which was my pay for the short time I was in the legion.

I signed some more documents then I was escorted off the camp in disgrace by two legionnaires. I was then put into an army jeep and taken to the train station. The jeep stopped, a door opened, I climbed out and without any words being spoken, they drove off.

My nightmare was over and so was my short career in the foreign legion. The train journey to Paris was a quiet one. I tried to erase the beatings and the attempted rape from my memories.

I can't remember much about the journey home but I never spoke about what happened in the foreign legion to anybody. I went home once again to my parents.

My mother was glad to see me and even my father had a smile on his face. My mother asked where I had been. I replied with a smile, "In the French Foreign Legion."

Chapter Forty-One

You're in the Army Now.

After all my escapades and troubles in foreign lands, I thought I had put a closure on that sort of thing but things were about to change.

One morning, while I was watching TV my mother and father came in to the front room. My father turned the TV off; my mother sat next to my father and he just came straight out with it

"Ian, you can't carry on in life with no purpose, getting into trouble with the police and being unemployed and just lazing about with your friends," he said.

"Tomorrow morning, your mother is taking you to the Army Recruitment Office in Great Moor Street Bolton."

"You're going in the army if you like it or not," my mother added. "It didn't do any of my brothers any harm and it will do you good and make you into a man."

I looked at my parents in complete horror and I shouted out, "You are joking. aren't you?"

I never told my parents what happened to me in the French Foreign Legion and I thought to myself there's no way I'm going to go through all that again.

She just kept repeating, "Ian I'm serious. You are going into the army; it will change your life for the better."

She put her arms around me and said, "Please Ian, do it for me. I'm worried about the direction you are taking in life. I don't want you to end up in prison."

I will never know why I agreed. It could only be because I loved my mother and I knew she cared about me.

In the morning, I got up and had breakfast. I was still hoping that she was joking but my smile was soon wiped off my face when she said. "Go and get dressed. We are going into Bolton to the Army Recruitment Centre."

I knew my mother was only doing what she thought was best me for me, so off we went. Even my sister Patricia came along.

I looked through the windows on the bus and I looked all around me and I muttered to myself that maybe it was a good thing to get away from Highfield and the troubles.

My mother held my arm and took me into the Army Recruitment Office and there in front of me was some kind of an officer in army uniform, sitting at his desk.

My mother told the officer this was her son and he wanted to join the army. If there would have been a hole in floor I would have dropped through it.

The officer told me sit down. He then asked me a few questions. "Have you been in trouble with the police?" to which my mother replied, "He's a good lad." This brought a huge smile to my face.

The officer told me, "There is much more to the army than military skill. You can go abroad. We will equip you with new skills, give you invaluable experience and develop strengths you didn't know you had."

He then asked me what qualifications I had. I replied that after I had left school I didn't take any exams. I went straight into a job.

Then the officer said you must take an entrance exam in English and Maths to see if we can accept you or not. This brought a huge smile to my face as I thought I was as thick as a barge pole and those were my two worst subjects.

I knew my chances of getting into army were slim so I was happy. My mother and sister then left as I had to do the test. The officer said, "You get thirty minutes per test, so take your time and good luck."

I made sure I would miss some of the questions out and answer a few of them wrong. I also made sure that I would finish the test-papers early.

The hour soon passed and the officer came back and took the test-papers from me. He said, "I won't be too long."

I was sure I was going to fail. The officer came back and said, "Congratulations you have passed." He shook my hand. I nearly collapsed with shock. I then signed some papers and I had just signed away three years off my life. My first thoughts were no more going to the football matches with my mates, no more women and my worst fears were remembering what happened in the French Foreign Legion.

The officer then told me I would be going to Sutton Coldfield Selection Centre for three days' assessment and I would also learn where they would be sending me.

I left the recruitment centre disheartened. I met my mother and sister in a cafe in the town centre.

I walked through the door and my mum shouted over, "Have you passed?"

I simply said, "Yes." My mum and my sister were overjoyed and they both hugged me.

I sat down and my mother said, "I didn't think you'd pass the entrance exams."

I mumbled under my breath, "I wish I hadn't."

My sister Pat held my hand and said, "I'm so happy for you. What would you like to drink?"

I laughed and said I would have a large whiskey which put a smile on both their faces.

I knew deep down she meant well and was doing her best for me. I told them both I had to go Sutton Coldfield Recruitment Centre for three days and I would be assessed there as to which army base and regiment I would be sent to.

"I have a week of freedom before I have to go and I'm going to enjoy myself before I leave," I replied.

My mother told the whole street I was going in the army and she was so proud of me. Everywhere I went people were patting me on the shoulder, to my dismay.

The time had arrived. I was on my way to Sutton Coldfield in Birmingham on a coach with some other recruits. The journey didn't take long, just a few hours. We arrived at the centre but the coach was stopped at the barrier where some army personnel checked the driver's papers. I was scanning around as I sat there. It just reminded me of the time I spent at Fort de Nogent in the French Foreign Legion and that brought a lump to my throat. I was trying to calm my fears by saying to myself, *I'm in the British army and I will be well treated*. We all got off the coach carrying our suitcases and were taken into a large room.

A lance-corporal introduced himself to us and explained all what would be happening while we were there for the next three days.

We were then taken into quarters where we would be sleeping or bunking up as the army recruits called it. Then we all went for meal in the canteen. There was lamb sirloin and lots of other great choices on the menu.

For some reason, I felt relaxed and the three years' service went to the back of my mind.

I got pally with a few of the lads including Sean from Manchester and Dale from Blackburn.

Both were football fans and that was my favourite subject. I had good laughs with them and we spent a lot time together over the three days.

Sean supported Manchester United and I let him know how much contempt I had for them. And Dale supported Blackburn rovers who I disliked as well but it was all in good fun and we laughed about the rivalries between us.

During our stay there, we had to do all kinds of physical tests, sit-ups and press–ups, general gym work and circuit work. We also did a written test and watched film shows about life in the army, and umpteen interviews.

At the end of the three days I was told I was going to be based at Strensall near York and that I was going into the Queens Lancashire regiment with a proud History going back as far 1689. It carried more battle honours on its colours than any other infantry unit in the Army. It was also able to proudly claim that it was the only regiment, from any army, ever, which had fought on every one of the World's inhabited continents.

The day had arrived Sean was coming along with me in to the Queens Lancashire Regiment. As for Dale, he was going into the Kings Own Regiment. The coach was ready. I said my goodbyes to Dale. I was on my way to Strensall army barracks to do three years in the army or so I thought. I was nearly twenty years old and I would be twenty-three when I came out of the army so I was still young enough to do the things I really wanted to do.

We arrived at Strensall army barracks in the late afternoon and as usual, we were stopped at the barrier by a soldier and then let through after our papers were found to be in order.

We were all taken into a large room and as usual, we were greeted by our block Lance-Corporal. I would later call him a bastard and that was the nick-name I used for him, while I served in the British army.

After being briefed we were shown to our sleeping quarters and beds were allocated so we knew where we would be bunking up.

We were also told the locations of the games room, the canteen etc. and the times we had our meals; also, what time we had to get up and what kind of training we were to receive and so on.

Getting up for breakfast was 6.15 and then back to barracks for a quick room inspection. Then we were out on parade at around 8.15 every day. All that did not go down too well with me.

I always looked forward to meal times and I must say the British army food was excellent. You could eat as much as you wanted from sirloin steak, lamb, every meat you could think of and the same with the desert. There was every cake you could think of and the ice-cream was out of this world.

My sleeping quarters were similar to the ones I had slept in, in the French Foreign Legion. The only difference was that it was a lot more modern and cleaner and not as many beds in each barracks.

I settled in pretty quickly on the first night and got on well with most people.

The morning soon came. It was lights on at 6.15; tidy your beds and then stand by your beds.

The Lance Corporal would check all the beds and the sheets had to have no creases in and be nicely squared. This would happen every morning without fail. As the days past my bed was frequently tilted over and the Lance Corporal would scream in my face because it wasn't good enough. Now and again I was forced to do press-ups until I got my bed right.

The day I was provided with all my army kit, my boots and my gym kit, I now felt like a real soldier and I did feel proud at the beginning.

The first six weeks were very much an introductory phase in the Infantry. They covered a multitude of subjects such as Values & Standards, Physical Training, and Skill at Arms lessons, drill and Field craft. This was a busy phase for me as recruits would remain in the barracks

It was very different from the French Foreign Legion. The British army was far more professional. You didn't get time to be bored as you were either doing interviews or gym work or physical training which I enjoyed very much.

I didn't see much bullying; only from the Lance Corporal who I called 'the bastard' with his big mouth. You had to be on your toes all the time with him.

The only altercation I had and it was only the once, was with a lad from Liverpool who was slagging me off because I was from Bolton. He gave me a little slap and I responded by punching him over his chair.

After four weeks, we were allowed to have a night out but we were pre-warned about not upsetting the locals by chatting up the local girls. Also, we must always stay in groups and not to walk back to base on our own. It turned out that many a soldier had had a good hiding from the locals; such were the bad feelings against us.

I always took advantage of my nights out enjoying the local girls company and I'm not ashamed to say I had a knee trembler on a few occasions on the way back to base.

I can honestly say it's true; girls do love a man in uniform.

On the odd occasion, I had been drunk and depending on who was on barrier duty, we usually managed to get through without any problems. Whenever I did guard duty, I would return the favour.

I only ever got in trouble once while on guard duty. That was when I forgot to salute an officer. I paid the price. I was left in the hands of 'the bastard,' my block Lance Corporal who derived great satisfaction from making me clean his boots over and over again; hence the name 'bastard.'

And on various occasions, if my uniform was not up to scratch or my bed or my army boots, 'the bastard' would have the shiniest boots on the camp.

I was longing to visit my home town to see my friends and family and the chance came. I got a week-end leave.

When my mother saw me in my uniform she cried. She told me she was very proud and that I looked a changed man, all grown-up she said.

I went out on the lash (piss-up) with my friends. They were telling me what was going on in the football games and all the trouble Bolton had had with Blackburn and Burnley and it had hurt our team up and down the country.

The more beer I drank the more home-sick I became. I missed all the football and all the fun that was attached to it.

It started to sink in that I was missing my freedom. I was naturally rebellious and I hated been told what to do

I felt suffocated and I blamed my father for turning me into the person I was.

The beatings over the years had taken their toll on me. I wanted to be happy and to be free and to have fun; all the things my father wouldn't let me be.

The weekend passed quickly and now I had to go back in the army. I started to resent it but I still went back on time.

The training became more intense. I was being shown more about how to use a rifle in shooting practice on the shooting range.

I did a few days away on what they called adventure training. We went rock-climbing and did other activities. I started to feel so homesick that my run-ins with the Lance Corporal I called 'the bastard' became more frequent. I was fed with all the marching and the early 6.15 starts. Everything was getting on top of me. I had had enough. I had only been in the army eleven weeks; just a few weeks away from passing out.

I decided it's was time to go home. I signed the necessary papers and I bought myself out of the British army.

I was proud of what little time I had in the army and I was very proud to serve my country. But I was rebellious. I just couldn't hack being told what to do. All my younger days I wasn't allowed to have friends, or girl-friends. I didn't know what was right or wrong. I was brought up with violence and suffered so many times at the hands of my father.

I thought fighting and being in gangs was normal. I didn't realise at the time I was on a path of self-destruction.

Chapter Forty-Two

Pastures New

At the age of eighteen I finally decided to leave Derwent Road and Farnworth for good and to put all the sadness and hurt and heartbreak behind me.

I wanted to forget seeing the constant reminders of the past in different parts of the house.

I wanted to forget the stairs my mum was dragged down, by my dad.

I wanted to forget the hallway where my dad tried to strangle my mother and would have succeeded but for the intervention of the police.

I wanted to forget the bathroom were my dad used to push my head under the water and where mother and I would wipe each other down from the blooded beatings we had received.

I wanted to forget my bedroom where my dad used to drag me out of bed, the same bed where I would hide under the covers, living in fear of my dad; the very same bed where I wet and soiled the sheets.

I wanted to forget the blood stains on my bedroom wall where he used to bang my head against the wall.

I wanted to forget the clock on the front-room wall where all the family used to watch the time and would live in fear of when he came home drunk from the bookies or the Flying Shuttle and would take his vengeance on my mum and me, if he had lost on the horses.

I wanted to get away from all this and start afresh to live a life with different surroundings and people. I just wanted to be happy and to be loved.

I woke up one morning and decided enough was enough. I got dressed and cleaned myself up in the bathroom. I looked in the very mirror where my mother would cover up our bruises with her make-up and listen to her words, ringing in my ears, "It stays in the family, Ian."

I sat on the toilet sobbing. I couldn't take it anymore. I wanted to forget the nightmares and the pain. Everywhere I looked there were painful memories.

Since the beating I gave my father, he was never the same. He never touched me or my mother again. It was my mother who now ruled the roost so I had no fears of leaving her behind. I went downstairs after I packed my small suitcase. It was early, which was a first for me.

I saw my father who just looked at me, put his head down and walked into the front room. I wanted to say goodbye but I just couldn't say it.

My mum was in the kitchen as usual, baking and cooking for the day's meals. She just looked at me, smiled and said, "I have been expecting this moment, Ian."

I went over to her and I held her tightly. I sobbed and told her I loved her more than anything in this world. I didn't stay for breakfast. I just said my goodbyes and left. I walked up the path and turned around. I could see my mum waving to me from the bedroom window. She was rubbing her eyes which made it obvious that she was crying. I wanted to go back in and comfort her but I had to stay strong.

I looked at the box-room window and the ledge where I used to climb down, to run away to play with my friends. I looked for the very last time and then I turned away and walked up Derwent Road, the very road where my dad used to chase my mum who was running for her life.

I walked past the very shops where I used to meet up with my friends and the Co-op where I used to steal bottles of cider, to drown my sorrows. I caught the red bus into Bolton. I sat upstairs with my head against the bus window with tears rolling down my face as the bus started to pull out. I passed the police house where Sergeant Swann used to live, the very house I graffitied and got my ultimate revenge. I turned around and I looked at my house on Derwent Road for the very last time, the house I called *the House on the Hill.*

Chapter Forty-Three

Time to say Goodbye

Me and family members celebrating my mum's life at Southfields (Bolton) after the funeral

On Saturday the 11th of June 2016 I was told that my mother had been admitted to hospital with infected pressure sores. She was in the Royal Bolton Hospital on ward A4. I visited her most nights. She was always smiling and said good things about the nurses who looked after her and always chatted to everybody who came on to the ward. She was given drugs to help heal the infection and I was confident she would be home soon. She still took pride in her appearance and even wanted her rollers in, such was the proud lady she was.

As the days went by, she gradually got worse. She was getting more pain now in her shoulder and her back. She started to complain about the severe pain she was in and was constantly complaining to the doctors and nurses who had to turn her over every two hours, to help heal the bed sores. But she was in agony and she started to dread the nurses coming into the ward.

The hospital visits were taking their toll on me. I started to cry every time I saw her. She would always look into my eyes and smile, as tears rolled down my face, just like she always did in my younger days when I was suffering at the hands of my father. She once held my hand and said to me, "Ian, I will always protect you."

I broke down and sobbed on her hospital bed. She rubbed my hair and said, "I will ways love you Ian." I was saved by the bell so to speak. It was time to go as it was the end of visiting. I kissed her on the cheek and said goodbye. I turned around and she blew me a kiss. I just carried on walking down the corridor crying my eyes out.

The next time I visited her she looked really ill. She now had a tube in her nose. It was oxygen to help lower her blood pressure. She was also now being given morphine to help her with the pain. She still smiled at me every time I visited, even though I could see she was suffering. Each time now when I visited her, doubts would start to creep in and I started worry that she would never come out of hospital again.

My worst nightmare would be confirmed. It was a Sunday. I visited as normal. I was just going into my mum's ward when I was stopped by a nurse and told to go into a room as she needed to speak to me about my mother. My worst fears were confirmed. I was told my mum's condition had deteriorated and that the next 24 hours were critical.

They needed permission from the next of kin not to resuscitate if it became necessary and I was also told she would not be put into intensive care.

I slumped onto a chair with my head in my arms and I started sobbing. I didn't want to lose my mum. I was totally devastated. My mum was put in to a side room. She had a heart monitor next to her bed. She still had the oxygen tube in her nose but she also had a tube in her leg for the morphine to help her with pain. In addition, she had tubes in her hands for the antibiotics and the fluid which eventually got into her lungs.

My mum was dying. All my siblings were now around her bed. The doctors only gave her 24 hours but my mum was a fighter. She would wake up now and again and smile at me which me made me feel worse. I would break down crying. She just looked into my eyes. I couldn't take it anymore. I had to go out of the room to console myself.

She survived the night and I started to get a bit of hope that she might live.

The next day I visited and the machine next to her bed was gone. The oxygen tube had been removed. She was now breathing through her stomach. My hopes of her surviving were dashed.

She would survive into the third day. All my siblings were now around her bed to say goodbye to her. I couldn't accept that she was dying. I held her hand and I decided I couldn't take it anymore. I couldn't look at her face knowing she was dying.

I went around the bed and I said goodbye to her. I was just going to kiss her cheek when she lifted her head, and opened her eyes. A tear ran down her cheek and then her head fell back onto her pillow. It really shocked me because it was the first time she had opened her eyes all day. It was as though she wanted to say goodbye to me, before I left.

I will never know the reason why, but that was the last thought I wanted to keep of her. I walked out of the hospital broken-hearted. That was the last time I saw her alive. Soon after, I received a phone call that she had died. It was Friday the 8th of July. I put the phone down and I sobbed. I slept all night with her picture in my hand.

On Friday, the 22nd July, it was the day of the funeral, time to say goodbye. The service was held at Overdale, at the crematorium. I carried my mum's coffin into the church and I kissed it twice. The room was full of family and friends. Next to the coffin was a picture of my mum which I couldn't stop looking at.

The service was beautiful. I was fine until they played the song that my mother loved, *Time to say Goodbye*, by Andrea Bocelli. I broke down and wept. I now realised that she was gone from my life. I felt totally empty inside. But for some reason I am not afraid to die anymore, as I know one day my mum will be waiting for me.

These poems are dedicated to the wonderful, brave lady who I am proud to remember as my mother.

Sound of Silence
I looked at her as she was sleeping.
The room was full of silence
I reached out and held her hand
The vision I had of her sleeping.
The rain drops on the window
Echoed in the room full of silence.
I held her in my arms as she passed away
I kissed my mum's cheek and whispered in her ear
I love you
The visions I had of her dying was seeded in my brain
And will always remain
In restless dreams, I walked alone

Narrow streets of cobbled stone
In completes silence I thought of her
All I have are the memories
Her pictures on my wall are all I have
My life will never be the same
How will I survive I do not know?
Her death will always haunt me.
Till the day we meet again
I will always walk this earth alone

Please don't Cry

Please don't say good bye
Please open your eyes.
Don't fade away from me
You are the greatest love of my life
Open your eyes and hold me in your arms

Please don't say good bye.
Stay close to me and open up your eyes.
Can't you see how much you mean to me.
Please hold on to your life
You mean so much to me
You are the greatest mum to me.

Please don't say good bye.

If you go away from me
You will be the brightest star in the sky
I will always keep my memories of you

My mother is a never- ending song in my heart.
In my heart and comfort, happiness and being.
I may sometimes forget the words but I always remember
the tune.

Mother

I can now longer see you with my eyes
Touch you with my hands
But I feel you in my heart for ever

The Sound of my Cries

I would wake up crying
I held out my arms
To be held and to be loved
Bad dreams of my father
I felt the hand of my father
Nightmares returned with a vengeance
Long and lonely nights
I cried a thousand tears
Nightmares and fears

The sound of my cries
Echoed through the night
Alone and afraid
I longed to be loved

The clock was ticking
Through the quiet night
I heard the footsteps coming
I knew my father was coming
I shut my eyes, hoping he would go away
I lay in the darkness quaking
Praying he would go away

The sound of my cries
Echoed through the night
The door opened, I opened my eyes
It was my mother, she held me so tightly
Wiping away the tears on my cheeks
She would rock me to sleep
She kissed my cheek, good night my love
I fell asleep

Motherly love

I cried for you
Mother
Sailing across the English Channel
All alone and afraid at fourteen
Running away from beatings and fears
I cried a thousand tears
Dad why oh why, do you hurt me?
Sailing across the deep blue sea
I waved good bye to the white cliffs of Dover
I longed for my mother's embrace
I cried for you
Mother

Paris

I arrived on foreign shores
Lost and alone
Afraid and fearful
Strange buildings, funny windows
Strange people, strange words.

Mother I miss you
Mother I need you
Strange inviting smells
Hungry and cold
All alone

Mother I miss you
Eiffel Tower, boats on the river Seine
Strange people, strange words
Free from the fists of my father
Fourteen and all alone

Mother I miss you
Afraid to go home
Fists are all that await me
Scared, hungry and afraid
Desperate and alone
I stole food and water to survive
Alleyways where I slept
Tears were my lullaby

Mother I miss you
I cried myself to sleep
I cried a thousand tears
Paris, thousands of people

All alone and afraid
All I wanted was love from my father
All that' awaits me is fists and tears
I cried a thousand tears

Mother I miss you
Please God make my father love me.
Caught by the police
Time to go home
I pray that I will be safe
All I want is to be held and to be loved

Why didn't you say you're sorry?

Why didn't you say you're sorry?
I felt your wrath your hand
The pain, the tears
I cried a thousand tears

Why didn't you say you're sorry?
The house full of violence and fears
I cried a thousand tears

I cried on my school desk
All alone and in pain I lived in fear
The clock tick-tock
The door opened
He was here

I felt your wrath, your hand
Blood, marks and tears
Shaking with fear
The nightmare was here

I ran away across land and sea
All alone and in fear
I returned to a house full of violence and fears
I cried a thousand tears

All I wanted was your love
Why didn't you say you're sorry?